OVERSIZE Thayer, Tom
978 The Missouri River
THAYER Country of Montana
and North Dakota

THE MISSOURI RIVER COUNTRY OF MONTANA AND NORTH DAKOTA

Published by "Montana Speaks"
307 Emerald Drive
Billings, Montana 59105

THE MISSOURI RIVER COUNTRY

OFFICE OF THE GOVERNOR
STATE OF MONTANA

Greetings:

We invite you to explore the Missouri River Country of Montana and
North Dakota. The Missouri River flows through landscapes as
diverse as the people who inhabit this land-deep canyons, wide-open
plains, majestic mountains, and towns both large and small.

Missouri River Country is a place where being a neighbor still means
more than simply living next to someone. Although we are separated
by vast stretches of land and many miles of river, we stay connected to
our neighbors both far and near, because in Montana and North
Dakota, we know we still need one another.

Enjoy your journey through this special corner of God's earth.

Sincerely,

MARC RACICOT
Governor

Author . . . . .Thomas N. Thayer

Photograpy . . . . .Thomas N. Thayer

Contributing Editor . . . . .Lucille Hill

Graphic Design . . . . .Barbara Scheppele

Assistant Editors . . . . .Marcy Thayer, Mary Ann Mackay

Geology Consultant . . . . .Henry Reed

Copyright applied for February, 1997

Copyright Number:

Library of Congress Number: 97-072082

ISBN Number: Hard Cover 0-9652439-2-3

Soft Cover 0-9652439-3-1

E-Mail: mtspeaks@wtp.net

Home Page: www.wtp.net/mtspeaks

Fax: (406) 245-9404

*Special thanks to Hall Diteman for allowing us
to reproduce many of his paintings in this book.*

Printed in the United States of America

Missouri River Country: 200 Years

VOLUME TWO

THE ROCKY MOUNTAIN SERIES

Contents

The old west used natural signs for travel.

Old Stone Face - Musselshell River

Rattlesnake Head - Missouri Breaks Country

Lizard Rock - Missouri backcountry

THE MISSOURI RIVER COUNTRY OF MONTANA AND NORTH DAKOTA

The Missouri River near Bismarck and Mandan, North Dakota. Lewis and Clark arrived here in October, 1804, spent the winter with the Mandan Indians. Later, across the river, were the riverboat ports and the town of Bismarck.

Prior to the Lewis and Clark Expedition of 1804 to 1806 no real knowledge of the upper Missouri River was available. No white explorers had been as far as the Yellowstone River confluence with the Missouri.

The Missouri River Country, a portion of the Louisiana Purchase, contained unknown quantities of rivers, streams, prairies, and mountains. The Missouri River Country spanned an area from the Rocky Mountains of Montana, Wyoming, and much of Colorado, eastward to the Mississippi River. This country is as varied as any found on the earth's surface. High, snow-capped mountains form the backbone, giving life to lakes, rivers, streams, grass, and deserts. This area and the Louisiana Purchase covered over 800,000 square miles of central North America.

EARLY IMPRESSIONS WERE NOT ACCURATE

Early writings about suggested routes for waterways across the North American continent were largely based on guesses or imaginary dreams. One published work written by Daniel Coxe in 1722, stated that in his opinion, "The Missouri River was navigable to its source. It would then be only a short ride by horseback to the westward flowing river."

Robert Rogers and Jonathan Carver first used the word "Oregon" sometime around 1765 and claimed the Indians told of a river flowing to the Pacific. Both proposed exploring expeditions. Captain Gray discovered the great Pacific river in 1792 and sailed up the main channel about 25 miles. He named this big river the *Columbia.*

These writings and events have been influential in early American history. Thomas Jefferson, our third president, was fascinated with this land. During the first year of his presidency, he began negotiations to purchase the Louisiana Territory which included the Missouri River Country. He realized this was great potential for continental expansion and the acquisition of this broad expanse of land would help in world influence.

EUROPEAN COUNTRIES AT WAR

In the early 1800's, Europe was in great turmoil and cared little about the affairs of the unknown middle North America. The beaver skins used to make gentlemen's hats were the main resource exported from this vast land...and the European influence was waning during these years.

JEFFERSON TAKING ADVANTAGE OF EUROPEAN PROBLEMS

The original intent of President Thomas Jefferson was to expand the United States to the Pacific Ocean. From current maps, Jefferson thought a waterway could be extended from the upper Missouri River to the Columbia River which would allow commerce to flow from the Atlantic Ocean to the Pacific Ocean. This would firmly establish the United States' influence from coast to coast.

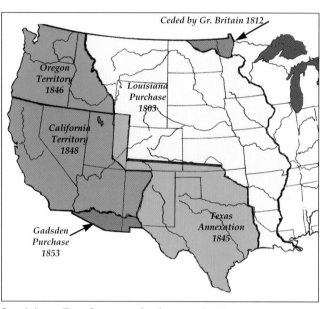

Louisiana Purchase, and other territories.

THE LEWIS AND CLARK EXPEDITION 1803-1806

Captain Meriwether Lewis, one of President Jefferson's secretaries, was placed in command of an expedition to explore the Missouri River from its confluence with the Mississippi River to the sources, then continue on to the Pacific Ocean. Captain Lewis selected William Clark to share the responsibilities of the exploration, and both would maintain a detailed journal. The expedition was to catalog new species of plants and animals, note resources, and attempt to find the best water route to the Columbia River. This notable event was con-

sidered the most outstanding accomplishment in the early history of this country. Gradually, after the expedition of 1804-1806, the vast resources of the Missouri River Country were exposed. The newly discovered riches included furs, and the Indian trade. Later came gold, copper, silver, timber, and land. Fur traders and trappers used the Missouri River to access the immense resource of beaver and other fur-bearing animals. They explored every tributary and rivulet throughout the Rocky Mountains. This continued to 1840, then came settlers, miners, homesteaders, and stockmen.

THE INDIAN OWNERSHIP VERSUS U.S. OWNERSHIP

After the Louisiana purchase from France, and the payment of $15 million dollars, Americans assumed the Louisiana Purchase was owned by the United States of America. Over a span of several hundred years, Indian tribes had been establishing ownership of these areas, and called this west their home. Conflict after conflict would result, creating many disputes with the American Indians over the next 80 years, as to who owned the land.

Each president succeeding Jefferson enacted his own political agenda and seemingly felt no obligation to honor the agreements of any previous administration. This proved unfortunate for the Indian tribes, as over 250 treaties were broken by the government of the United States. Each change or reversal of a treaty agreement fostered continued contempt for the rights of the American Indian. How-

Courtesy of Mandan Museum.

Chief Four Bears of the Mandan Indians. The Mandan, Hidatsa, and the Arikara tribes were friendly and helpful to Lewis and Clark as they spent the winter in close proximity.

cities, and belching smoke stacks. This opened up the west, and harvesting the resources helped to establish the United States as a new and powerful country.

THE GEOLOGICAL HISTORY BOOK

The Missouri River Country is an open geologic history book, with chapters dating back to the Pre-Cambrian exposures in the Beartooth Mountains. In fact, fossils of most geologic periods have been discovered in the Missouri River country. These geologic exposures revealed an array of resources possibly unparalleled in the world. Cement is made from the limestone deposited during the Mississippian and Pennsylvanian periods. In some areas, swamps with massive plant growth formed thick coal beds, oil and gas deposits. During the Mesozoic Era, plants, animals, insects, birds, and other life evolved into thousands of different species. While these

ever, one constant remained...the United States would become one country from the Atlantic to the Pacific.

EARLY AMERICANS WERE DESTRUCTIVE

During the relatively brief time between 1805 and present day, the topography has been drastically altered, Grassy plains, forests, and natural hills changed to barbed-wire fences, plowed fields, dredged-out river bottoms, and holes in the earth. Railroad lines and spurs were built extending service along most major routes. The area was punctuated with towns,

North Dakota was cold winter country. The Indians built houses of poles and sod and spent winters here. In the home they kept the extended family of aunts, uncles, horses and dogs. During the summer they raised corn, squash and beans for winter food.

changes occurred in time blocks of millions of years, it was relatively sudden in geologic time.

During the late Cretaceous Period, mountain

The North American buffalo were to the Indians like cattle of today. The difference, the buffalo needed no care and the Indians hunted when the herds came near.

the Missouri River system. Between the Rocky Mountains and the Atlantic Ocean, the land under the inland seas began rising above sea level. Major erosive forces went to work transporting materials from the mountains to the lowlands. Vast swamps of dense vegetation were created as the seas were shut off and pushed back to the oceans.

building occurred in many areas of the world. In the Missouri River Country, the Rocky Mountains were forming. The mountain laramide orogeny (mountain building) changed the climate and topography, creating

During this period, the splitting of the earth's crust was happening along the stress lines where the Pacific plate was meeting the Continental plate. Volcanoes occurred, spewing volumes of cinder, ash, and lava continually forming new terrain. As the plates continued compression, the forced uplifting and faulting

The Rocky Mountains, west of Fort Benton, were high with steep walls. The earth's crust had buckled forming a ridgeline the full length of North America.

The only way for goods to arrive from the east coast to the Pacific coast was by ship around South America. This was costly and dangerous. The railroads opened up the west giving the United States an "inland water route".

A train load of materials traveling up the Missouri River on the way toward points west and the Pacific coast cities.

created the beautiful and scenic Missouri River country. Later, glaciers and erosion carried soils to form alluvial flats, adding "frosting" to the landscape.

The compression of the plates tilted strata, formerly buried deep in the earth's crust. Some were tilted to nearly vertical positions, exposing gold, silver, zinc, platinum, palladium, copper, and other minerals. Gold was discovered in the 1860's, and the news rumbled across the land. The thundering hordes of miners came by any means available to feverishly attack the landscape. The Rocky Mountains were a source of riches in minerals and metals, water for irrigation, alluvial flats for farm ground, and wild game numbering in the millions. The Missouri River Country has been transformed many times throughout geologic history. However, in less than one hundred years, man has altered this landscape beyond the ability of natural changes.

Thomas Jefferson dreamed of a waterway to the Pacific and eighty years later, the dream was fully realized in two iron rails that stretched from the east coast to the Pacific. The railroad opened up the West, bringing homesteaders who would build cities with churches and schools. The railroads transported machinery and other goods westward, returning with beef, grain, metals, timber, and other products. The west changed overnight from an isolated landscape to one housing millions of people...people coming from all parts of Europe and in the mix were other nationalities including Chinese and Africans.

The Missouri River Country, with its railroads, became the back yard of the eastern industrial establishment. The rich western farms yielded a continuous flow of cheap food to the workers. A young nation of fewer than 200 years, became a world power overnight.

The nomadic Indians did not fit well into this potpourri of Norwegians, Germans, Italians, and other Europeans seeking a new life. Immigrants came to this country to take over and claim ownership. They had fled oppressive governments in Europe, and in the name of freedom took away the same commodity from the American Indians.

That was yesterday. Today, scarred as the Missouri River Country is by old mining operations, barbed-wire fences, plowed ground, and cities, the opportunities are still here—different, but here. Unlimited recreation attracts visitors from all over the world, to visit Glacier and Yellowstone Parks. People come to live where the view includes a clear stream or silhouetted mountain against a blue sky.

This volume illustrates views of how geography and geology affect history.

These sciences dictate the activities man entertains for livelihoods. Along with these activities comes the politics of each era, and often the mode is greed.

Early Missouri Country

The beauty of the Missouri River near Great Falls symbolizes the wealth of resources a river gives to the country.

The early history of the Missouri River Country played an important part in the development of the United States of America. The following pages attempt to correlate how geologic happenings create geography and how geography dictates history. The development of resources give life to the people and reason for their continued existence.

CHAPTER 1
The Missouri River Country History

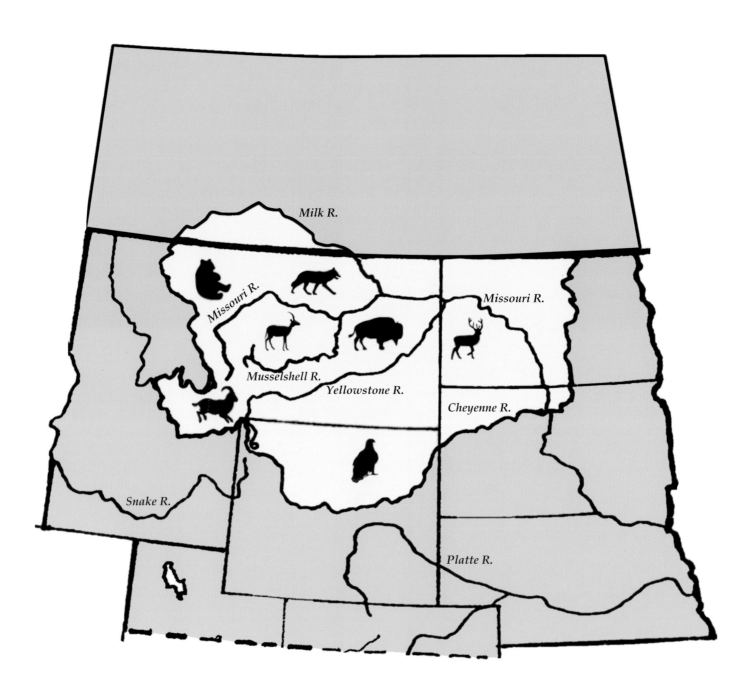

Milk R.

Missouri R.

Missouri R.

Musselshell R.

Yellowstone R.

Cheyenne R.

Snake R.

Platte R.

Missouri River Country

Influence Area

The history of the Missouri River Country began with the creation of the Rocky Mountains which in turn spawned the Missouri River system. The geology, volcanics, earthquakes, erosion and glaciers, continues to shape these lands today. The mountains changed the climate and the plants and animals rearrange their lifestyles to match. Today we are looking at the Missouri River Drainage and the influence areas.

Thomas Jefferson held high regards for his part in the Lewis & Clark Expedition. In his Monticello home in Virginia, still on display, are buffalo, deer, and elk heads, and a variety of Indian artifacts collected from 1804 to 1806. These specimens were the first seen by Americans and started the intrigue to visit the West.

Thomas Jefferson, third president of the United States of America, was a philosopher, writer, and naturalist. One of the greatest visionaries of his time, Jefferson could foresee a country stretching from the Atlantic coast to the Pacific Ocean. This country, with an inland water route for commerce, was a dream others did not share at this time. Most politicians and leaders were absorbed with problems closer at hand.

To realize this dream, Jefferson needed to acquire the territory called the Louisiana Country. He commissioned Captain Meriwether Lewis, one of his secretaries, to begin preparation for an exploratory trip up the Missouri River. They knew the area to be part of the Mississippi basin and encompass the Missouri drainage. Originally, the plans were to travel up river to find a water route to the great Columbia River flowing to the Pacific.

During the first year of preparation, Spain owned the rights to the Louisiana Territory, but deeded those rights over to France. Nearly broke from the long war with England, France was eager to entertain a sale to the United States, and for $15 million dollars, the United States gained 800,000 square miles of new territory. The topography and resources of this area were unknown; however, for less than three cents per acre, the boundaries of the United States doubled.

Captain Meriwether Lewis and his chosen companion, Captain William Clark, now had a real purpose in being the first explorers to travel the Missouri River Country. In 1803, after much study, preparations for the trip were completed. Bull boat frames were made, tools and guns tested, and procedures were established to document new plants and animals. Detailed records were kept in the now famous Lewis and Clark journals.

1737	Le Sieur De La Verendrye, French fur trader, contacts the Mandan Indian's fur trade
1753	French and Indian War - forcing some Indian tribes to migrate west
1776	American Revolutionary War against England
1783	Revolutionary War ends
1803	Louisiana Purchase
1804	Lewis and Clark spend winter at Knife River with Mandan, Hidatsa, Minitarees
1807-1840	Fur trade and trapping - Yellowstone River Country of Montana, Wyoming
1830-1883	Riverboat era on the Missouri River
1847	Start of Oregon Trail
1862	Gold ... Grasshopper Creek, southwestern Montana Territory
1863	Bozeman Trail
1870's	Copper mining - Butte, Anaconda
1869	Railroad arrives Bismarck, N.D.
1863	Bismarck, N.D. incorporates as a city
1883	Railroad connects through Montana Territory to Portland, Oregon
1883	Homesteading North Dakota
1889	Montana and North Dakota statehood
1900-1916	Homesteading Montana
1916-	Barbed wire shuts off free range
1914-1918	World War I
1929	Great Depression
1941	World War II
1951	Korean War
1964	Vietnam War

The expedition started in earnest after spending the winter with the Mandan Indians at the Knife River confluence with the Missouri, 40 miles north of what is now Bismarck, North Dakota. The group was visited almost daily by the Indians, drawing maps on animal skins to help the Americans travel into the unknown world called the Missouri River Country.

SACAJAWEA

During the trip from St. Louis to Mandan, one soldier died from fever, reducing the group to thirty three. Lewis and Clark decided to take with them a French-Canadian named Charbonneau and his wife, a sixteen-year-old Shoshone Indian girl, as guides and interpreters. This proved a very wise decision. The Indian girl, known as Sacajawea, has been forever revered as one of America's great women.

Although Charbonneau spoke only French, Sacajawea understood the Indian language and conversed with her husband in Minitarees. She would sign the Indian message to her husband, and he in turn would translate in French to the one man of the expedition who could speak both French and English. The four-way system was vital to ensure the success of the expedition.

A replica of a keel boat that the expedition pulled up river.

The fleet-footed antelope was one of the first new species encountered by the expedition.

In March 1805, the expedition pushed off with canoes and a keel boat from the Mandan, Hidatsa, and Arikara Indian villages to begin travel up the unknown river called the Missouri. They knew of the buffalo, but were surprised at the increasing number and size of the herds as they traveled west. Deer, antelope, coyotes, wolves, and grizzly bears were in great abundance. Herds of elk grazed along the stream banks and grassy flats. The food supply seemed limitless and the explorers ate well through the first half of the trip.

THE RUGGED MISSOURI BREAKS

The river was flat and winding through North Dakota but arriving into the Missouri Breaks of Montana, the river evolved into a canyon with steep wooded ravines. During the Bull Lake Ice Age, the glaciers stopped the river from flowing north to the Hudson Bay. The river course changed to flow east to join the Mississippi and formed a rugged young canyon. During earlier geologic times, the Yellowstone volcanoes were spewing major volumes of ash and cinder. The Missouri River drainage collected cubic yards of this material which eventually formed the new Missouri Breaks of clay hills, gullies, and rough land hidden away from the world ... now called The Missouri Breaks back country..

Early American maps and Indian skin maps indicated small "humps" rising from the distant prairies. However, when Lewis and Clark arrived at what would become Fort Benton, Montana, these mountains, ghosts in the distant sky, rose up to twelve thousand feet above sea level. It was an awesome sight to the thirty-four men rowing and pulling their twenty-six foot keel boat upstream. By now, they had traveled over 2,000 miles since leaving St. Louis. None of the journey so far would compare to the difficulty in traversing the Rocky Mountains. The seemingly best route was to follow the Missouri as far as possible before abandoning their boats and continuing their journey on horseback.

All information available gave no hint as to the height and distance across the Rockies.

The Lower Falls of the upper Missouri River was a spectacular scene when Meriwether Lewis walked up river and caught his first view. It was here that a grizzly bear chased Captain Lewis into the river.

On the upper Beaverhead River, the Shoshone Indians were found and trading for horses began.

FIRST FALLS ON THE MISSOURI

Soon after leaving the Fort Benton area, they found the "Great Falls" of the Missouri, as the Indians had described. Here they embarked on a two week, eighteen mile portage. Finally, nearly the first of August, they were able to continue up river to what is now known as Three Forks. Captains Lewis and Clark named the middle fork The Madison, after James Madison, the east fork The Gallatin after Secretary Gallatin, and the west fork The Jefferson after President Thomas Jefferson.

By now, they had traveled for five months since leaving the Mandan villages without seeing other humans. Finding Sacajawea's people was becoming increasingly important as the Shoshone owned horses. Soon, they would need to stash their boats and continue by horseback if the expedition was to be successful. While camping at the mouth of the Jefferson River, they decided to continue up the west fork until the river forked three times again. Both Lewis and Clark were becoming somewhat apprehensive about locating the Shoshone Tribe. When the expedition reached the area now called Twin Bridges, they chose the middle fork, given the name Beaverhead by the Shoshone Indians. In this broad, expansive country, it seemed unlikely they would find the Shoshone Indians. Even so, about fifty or sixty miles up the Beaverhead, they happily found Sacajawea's people. Their expedition was rejuvenated by acquiring the needed horses in exchange for goods.

CAMPING WITH THE SHOSHONE INDIANS

After several days of discussion, map making, and trading, the expedition headed up Lemhi Creek Pass and turned northward to Lolo Pass where they would follow an old Indian trail to the Clearwater River. Several days later, an early August snowstorm nearly claimed their lives. Upon reaching the Clearwater, the Nez Perce Indians offered them salmon and roots. It saved their lives, but the fare made them ill and here they rested for several days before traveling the Clearwater to the Snake River. The expedition party switched from horseback to canoes, and then followed the Snake River to the confluence of the Columbia River. Several Indian groups were encountered on the way.

FINDING THE PACIFIC OCEAN

The Columbia River Indians helped guide the party to the Pacific Ocean, arriving November 8, 1805. Three years had elapsed when Lewis and Clark finally hoisted the American flag at Fort Clatsop on the south side of the mouth of the Columbia River. They spent a rainy winter at the fort, and in the spring of 1806, started the return trip home.

This notable journey, completed against all odds by Captains Lewis and Clark, extended the American influence from the Atlantic coast to the Pacific Ocean. Thomas Jefferson's dream of an inland waterway was delayed by eighty years, but came in a way of the railroad. The iron horse traveling on steel rails would establish the method of transporting goods from coast to coast.

American history has paid many tributes to Lewis and Clark and crowned the Indian woman Sacajawea first lady. Thomas Jefferson, the statesman, proved once again how strong the early American leadership was in molding this country.

Looking down the railroad track is much like taking an endless trip into time. The railroads transformed the west overnight from frontier to rural America.

This stately old Limber Pine, is showing the character of it's 500 year fight against Montana winters, standing high on a rock y ridge.

NEW PLANTS AND ANIMALS

Lewis and Clark were instructed to write daily journals, draw maps, and gather plant and animal species to be brought back to Washington. When the expedition arrived at the Mandan villages, one boat was sent back to St. Louis with a variety of plants and animals. Animals like prairie dogs were sent back alive in cages.

The countryside changed from deciduous forests to cottonwood groves, to grass, then sage and desert, and then back to grass. As they ascended the mountains, new varieties of trees were found: ponderosa pine, limber pine, Douglas fir, spruce, and cedars along with many new species of flowering and bush-type plants. With so many new species, the group could not begin to catalog all this new world, but Meriwether Lewis found the bitterroot flower, now the state flower of Montana. The Eastern Botanical Society named this beautiful plant and flower after him, the Bitterroot Lewisia.

These species can all be found for study and viewing: the prairie flowers of the prickly pear cactus, small lilies, and the beautiful yucca.

The Montana State flower was named the Bitterroot Lewisia in honor of Captain Meriwether Lewis.

Two Prairie Dogs were sent to President Jefferson.

Blooming in profusion from May through July, the flowers grace the prairies, rocky hillsides and mountain flats from St. Louis to the Rocky Mountains. The variety would dazzle a botanist as one flower group after another colors the clear alpine panorama.

THE INDIANS MADE USE
OF MANY PLANTS

Indians knew well the uses of plants. They dug roots, gathered leaves, fruits, and berries as a major part of their diet. Today, diets would be more healthful if we used more Indian lore in plant food use.

Blackfeet Indian women carried an animal skin bundle in which were found items such as an eagle wing bone, herbs, twisted grass, hair, the tail of a small creature, seeds, etc. They believed the bundle was a spirit, bringing good luck and other things. The ability of the Indian to live with nature was a skill the whites could have studied more, but it was felt the Indian's mythology was incompatible with Christianity.

At first, Lewis and Clark scoffed at Indian stories about the grizzly bear, but after several close encounters, they soon realized just how dangerous the big brown really was. The Indians called the buffalo their spirit animal because of the many uses the people could make of the buffalo. The grizzly, however, was the most feared and it took great bravery to kill one. The wolf was considered the most intelligent and the medicine man would often wear a wolf skin when conducting rituals. The animals, plants, weather, moon, and the sun were the world of the Indians. Their surroundings were of great importance.

Dances and festivities were all part of the preparation for hunting, raiding, marriage ceremonies, and other important activities.

A new species, the Rocky Mountain bighorn sheep, was first seen in the Missouri Breaks of northern Montana.

Skins of the western coyote were sent back to the naturalists.

Magpies, a member of the crow family, fascinated members of the expedition.

The largest member of the deer family is the North American Moose found throughout the Rocky Mountains into Canada and Alaska. The animal stands 7 feet at the shoulders and matures out weighing 2,500 pounds.

Lewis and Clark found the elk to be prairie animals in the 1805 expedition. Later, under intense hunting pressure, the elk changed their habitats to mountain canyons.

The Indian History

The herds of wild game were large and numerous and there seem to be no end to the resource. These animals had few natural enemies for thousands of years and evolved into certain patterns of travel, feeding and habitat.

During the late 1860's pressure by white Americans nearly brought many species to extinction. Better management of hunting and habitat have changed these number to positive counts at the end of this century.

Many animals have moved closer to cities and have adapted to new environments, and others have changed from prairies to mountains.

Migrations from summer ranges to winter ranges have been altered for many big game animals.

The changes that happened over millions of years were slow. The accelerated growth of western America from the 1880's created havoc because many species of animals could not adapt rapidly.

CHAPTER 2
The Indian History

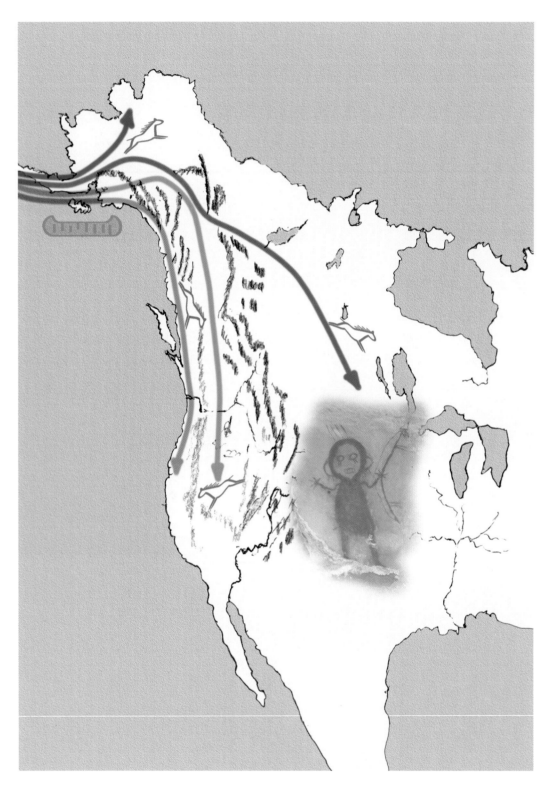

The Asian migration across the Bering Straits occurred over a period of years, and these people became the Native Americans. Gradually, the migrations formed many different tribes scattered from Alaska to southern South America.

Anthropologists believe the American Indians migrated across the Bering Straits from Asia when the oceans were lower. These groups spread downward and Eastward to occupy both North America and South America.

AMERICAN INDIANS OF THE MISSOURI RIVER COUNTRY

The first known inhabitants of the Missouri River Country were the Paleo Indian tribes prior and during the glacial Ice Age. Anthropologists have only hints of their existence. Several migrations of Asians crossed the Bering Straits from 30,000 to 15,000 years ago and some possibly later. These early people were to become the foundation of Indian tribes from Alaska to South America.

Some tools such as spear points have been found. The discovery of a mammoth elephant kill pit near Worland, Wyoming, the charcoaled caves of the Pryor Mountains, and the ceremonial wheel on top of the Bighorn Mountains support evidence of Indian life before our modern Indians. During the Glacier Era, there is a gap with limited evidence of the Indian presence in the Missouri River Country. The modern day Mandan, Hidatsa, Arikara, Sioux, Assiniboine, Gros Ventre, Blackfeet, Cree, Crow, and other Indians evolved from the migration of Algonquins from the eastern part of the United States. They seemed to have no knowledge of the Paleo Indians of earlier times who lived in the Missouri River country.

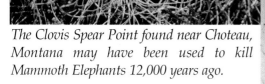

The Clovis Spear Point found near Choteau, Montana may have been used to kill Mammoth Elephants 12,000 years ago.

Early Paleo Indians may have built fires leaving charcoal in the Pryor Mountain Caves thousands of years ago.

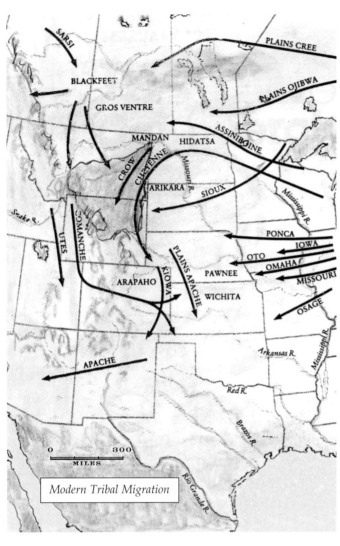

Modern Tribal Migration

The modern Indians migrated into the Missouri River Country from northeastern America.

The first Americans to enter the Missouri River country were Lewis and Clark in 1804. They met the Teton Sioux while traveling up the Missouri during the summer. This was a hostile situation with the war-like Sioux. The Indians who preferred odds in their favor saw members of the expedition holding guns and boats with mounted guns on their bows. This show of power produced a peaceful meeting with trading and pipe smoking.

When Lewis and Clark arrived at the Knife River villages of the Mandan, Hidatsa, Arikara and the Minitarees (Gros Ventre), they found friendship and help. These Indians were a combination of agriculturists and hunters. The Mandans raised corn, squash, beans, pumpkins, and the Minitaree hunted buffalo, elk, deer, and antelope. These tribes all traded among themselves. The Indians of the west were great travelers and traders, coming from many miles away to parlay for goods.

The Missouri River flowing through the Breaks with the Bearpaw Mountains in the background.

The Native Americans used many methods to hunt buffalo. Bluffs in the Missouri River Country were used to drive buffalo herds to their death on the rocks below.

courtesy of the Buffalo Bill Historical Museum, Cody, WY

THE EARLY YEARS

During the early 1700s, the population of the Mandan villages was estimated to be 10,000. Following the smallpox epidemic of 1778, their numbers were reduced to 4,000. The dwindling population was the basic reason for the Arikara, Hidatsa, and the Mandans to move their villages in close proximity. This gave them the ability to ward off the marauding Sioux Indians of the south.

The first European to trade with these Indians was LeSieur De La Verendrye in 1738. This established a constant fur trade, first with the French and later with the British. Trading introduced guns, knives, tools, beads, and blankets to these tribes. During this time, the European fur and animal skin market was flourishing, especially beaver pelts for European hats. When Lewis and Clark arrived and announced this was now American land, French and British traders were not happy.

However, Lewis and Clark promoted peace and assured them trade would continue as usual. This peace was generally accepted for many years and trading was not disrupted.

THE SPRING OF 1805

The Lewis and Clark expedition proceeded up the Missouri River during the spring of 1805. They detected many Indian sign, but saw no other humans until they met the Shoshones at the headwaters of the Beaverhead River. They traveled through Yankton Sioux and Assiniboine country near the mouth of the Yellowstone, through Crow country, and finally through Blackfeet country of the Marias River.

Sacajawea's appearance at the Shoshone's camp created happiness among the Shoshones. She helped with making a good trade for needed horses. Sacajawea was able to accomplish the same with the Nez Perce and

Piegan Cheif... Two Guns Whitecalf

the river Indians along the lower Snake and Columbia rivers. The river Indians were helpful, guiding the party westward to the mouth of the Columbia. While all these Indians developed different cultures, there remained many similarities. Using sign language, Sacajawea could translate, tell Charbonneau, and he could relate the information to Captains Lewis or Clark.

THE RETURN TRIP

When the party returned to the Mandan villages, they persuaded one of the Mandan Chiefs, Shehake, to travel back to Washington to visit with President Jefferson. Chief Shehake and his companions found the east full of great spirits but when they returned home in 1809 and related what they had seen on their trip, they were badly ridiculed. Those who stayed at home could not believe the tales of streets, lights, ships in harbors, and horse carriages.

THE STRONG TRIBES OF
THE UPPER MISSOURI

The Crows of the Yellowstone River country and the Blackfeet of Marias and Milk River country were the strong tribes of the upper

Missouri. The Blackfeet were comprised of three tribes: Piegans, Bloods, and Blackfeet. Because of their isolation, these tribes were not affected by the first epidemic of smallpox. All of these tribes became better nomadic hunters when they acquired the horse, which they called the "spirit dog." The Crows acquired the horse about 1730, while the Blackfeet were one of the last to acquire the horse. Once the horse was part of their culture, obtaining food became easier and the Indian populations increased.

The Blackfeet were strong in numbers and raiding parties plundered throughout Montana and Canada. They were feared by both Whites and Indians from Canada to the Salt Lake country and into the Crow country of the Yellowstone River. The Crow and Blackfeet were old enemies, raiding and stealing both horses and women whenever possible. While the Sioux did travel north of the Missouri, they generally stayed in South Dakota, eastern Wyoming, and the Tongue-Powder River country.

This map illustrates the times that the different tribes acquired the horse.

The Indians acquired horses from the Spanish who brought them from Spain in the early 1500's.

Following the Lewis and Clark Expedition came the American Fur Company with fur traders and trappers. These expeditions, led by Manuel Lisa and General Ashly, concentrated on the upper Yellowstone River country. The Blackfeet were so fierce, most trappers avoided the Missouri Breaks, the Marias River, Sun River and the upper Missouri. The Missouri Fur Company tried to move into the Three Forks area of the upper Missouri about 1810 to 1811 but the Blackfeet killed, stole, and drove these Americans out. This lasted for some 12 to 15 years before fur trappers attempted another venture into this area.

THE BLACKFEET

The Blackfeet culture was simple, yet complicated. Their way of life was hunting buffalo and other game. They also gathered berries, roots, herbs, wild peas, parsnips, wild turnips, prickly pear cactus, buds, and rose hips. On occasion they were able to trade with the Mandans for beans, squash, and corn.

The whites considered the Indians "ignorant and backward", but in reality their lifestyle was well suited to this area of North America. They were a hardy nomadic group and could withstand the harsh northern climate far better than the French, English, or Americans.

The Indians observed many rituals in their society, some religious, and others allowing transition from childhood to adulthood. Their lifestyle was not well understood by the White Europeans. The Indian nation would have war chiefs, peace chiefs, and medicine chiefs, all with a voice in the council. There were various other societal standings for both men and women.

The ability to make decisions was often encumbered because of the way actions were voted by the councils. These customs were difficult for the whites to comprehend. An Indian man who had distinguished himself in war or hunts would often form a separate band or tribe of his own. These bands would travel as a small unit into other areas, yet the group would still remain part of the whole nation of Blackfeet. When a chief of a tribe would agree to the whites' wishes, the military establishment would take this as a consenting decision for all the tribes while perhaps other chiefs had voted the opposite.

Indians measured their intelligence by their ability to hunt, to war, to steal horses, to protect and care for the family, and how to recognize places to camp that would offer the best protection during winter.

The Blackfeet Indians were a powerful nation with large bands or groups able to defend their area from the Cree, the Crow, the Canadians and the Americans for many years. They raided throughout central Canada, northern Montana Territory, south throughout the west side of the Rocky Mountains, and under the shadow of the Grand Tetons. Blackfeet Indian women often fought alongside their husbands or after their husband's death. Two of these warrior Indian women were "Elk Hollering in the Water" and "Pitamahtan (Running Eagle)." Both were famous for their bravery and horsemanship.

Many Indian medicine men used wolf skins in their rituals. The American Indians believed the wolf was the most intelligent of animals.

Americans attempted again in 1823 but their trapping venture ended with 24 trappers killed and a large number of traps, supplies, and guns lost to the war parties of the Blackfeet. The Americans backed away from the beaver-rich country of the Upper Missouri. Then, a sudden decline in beaver fur prices stopped fur trapping in 1840. The result was a reprieve from the invasion of trappers for the next 10 to 15 years.

THE GOLDEN PERIOD

The period between 1730 and 1850 was the most prosperous time for the Blackfeet. They first acquired the horse, some say, from surprising a group of Spaniards, scaring them into the rocks, and gleefully leading the mules and horses to their camp. This possibly occurred in the California country. The next historical event seemed to have occurred when Captain Lewis, while exploring the Marias River drainage, managed to outfight a small group of Blackfeet warriors trying to steal their guns and horses. From that time there existed a three-way rivalry among the British, Blackfeet, and American trappers. Their constant hostility was a major problem for the American Fur Company. The Americans were sworn enemies of the Blackfeet. Again, in 1823, the American Fur Company tried to enter Blackfeet country. Americans had not ventured into the upper Missouri tributaries since the incident with John Colter and John Potts at Three Forks of Montana Territory. During this encounter, John Potts was killed and Colter had a 250-mile run for his life.

The Mandan, Arikara, and Hidatsa Indians raised corn, squash, and beans. Native Americans from the Missouri River Country would come to trade for these foods.

THE OPENING OF THE OREGON TRAIL

Finally, Jedediah Smith found a route through the south pass over the Rockies which became the Oregon Trail. After the opening of the Oregon Trail in 1847, the steady stream of settlers and then gold miners soon overran the country. The American military was sent to protect the whites from the Blackfeet and other tribes.

The first American treaty with the Blackfeet was negotiated with Lame Bull, Chief of the Blackfeet in 1855. The chief relinquished half of their hunting ground in exchange for $20,000 in goods and $15,000 for Christian education to be paid each year to the tribe. Governor Stevens of the Washington territory and Alexander Culbertson, bourgeois of Fort Benton, negotiated this treaty with the Nez Perce, Flatheads, Spokane, Blackfeet, Cree Assiniboine and others; giving the Indians two citizenships. 1) citizenship in the United States of America and 2) sovereignty of their own lands. However, the second payment of goods by the American government consisted of spoiled food, broken wagons, moth-eaten blankets, rusty guns, and whiskey.

THE KILLING OF THE VAST HERDS OF BUFFALO

During this time, the market hunters were killing the buffalo by the thousands, taking only hides and tongues. This slaughter was encouraged by the U.S. government, and forced the Indians into a submissive, starving mode. Broken treaties, smallpox epidemics, whiskey, and near extinction of the buffalo proved disastrous for the strong, proud Blackfeet tribes of the Missouri Country. After 1855, it wasn't long before the Americans were in control of the Missouri River Country of Montana.

The buffalo was everything to the Indians: food, hides, and tools. With the horse, the Indians were able to hunt more efficiently.

The two most famous Native American women were Pocahontas and Sacajawea. Sacajawea served as guide and interpreter to the Lewis and Clark Expedition. Captain Lewis bestowed on this woman many accolades.

Amber Old Horn is a young Crow woman living in Hardin, Montana. Her image is similar to our heroine of the Lewis and Clark Expedition. The difference is 200 years and a completely different society both for the Native American women and the White Americans.

During the years of Sacajawea of the Shoshone Indians, the Indian woman's role was childbearer, clothes maker, food gatherer, camp mover, etc., but her life was structured and she shared the rituals of her societies. The Indian men were part of the tribe and all were working together.

Today the Native American woman is expected to become educated, work in the White society, and bear the children. Her burden is different because of a different society, but the Native American male often doesn't fill the role of protector, father, or meat provider of the early tribal structure.

While, as a nation, we quickly immortalized Sacajawea, our modern society does not help Amber Old Horn enjoy the status as a viable young woman. Her social and economic situation does not provide enough prestige for full absorption into this economy. Having a job and making a living is still the number one endeavor to the adjustment of living in the United States of America. In this character, the Indian woman is left behind.

Amber Old Horn

SACAJAWEA

Sacajawea, a Shoshone Indian woman, was guide and interpreter for the famous Lewis and Clark exploration from 1805 to 1806. Still revered by the American people, her image has been romanticized into heroism beyond and above other women in American history. Her name has graced hotels, bridges, schools and buildings spanning an area from St. Louis to Portland, Oregon. Honorary brass plates with her name engraved are set in stone, and found along the famous Lewis and Clark route.

TOUSANT CHARBONNEAU

Sacajawea's tribe of Shoshone Indians lived in the headwater area of the Beaverhead,

Big Hole, and Ruby rivers. As a young girl of thirteen, Sacajawea's people were raided by a Minitarees hunting party. Sacajawea was stolen and taken to a faraway village where she was a slave for about three years. A French Canadian fur trader, Tousant Charbonneau, saw her and began a trade for her hand in marriage.

Charbonneau took his new wife to the Indian villages of the Mandans, Arikara, and Hidatsa near the Knife River confluence with the Missouri River. Here she was living and gave birth to her first child, called Pomp.

LEWIS AND CLARK EXPEDITION 1805

The Lewis and Clark Expedition arrived during October 1804, and asked to spend the winter with the Mandan Indians. After council and trading, they were welcomed, and proceeded to build a fort in the cottonwood trees one mile downstream, called Fort Mandan.

During this winter, the Indians and whites spent a great deal of time talking, planning, and map making for the expedition upriver into the unknown Missouri River country. It was soon noted that Sacajawea could talk with the Indians. Her husband, Charbonneau, could in turn speak French with a member of the expedition who spoke both French and English. The relationship worked well and Lewis and Clark decided to hire Charbonneau and Sacajawea to accompany them on the trip as interpreters and guides. Sacajawea, the daughter of a Shoshone Chief, was willing as she saw this as a means to return to her people.

Lewis and Clark considered Sacajawea valuable as she would be able to talk with the Shoshones and help trade for horses. Historians likely gave her more credit for guiding than she earned, but she was able to work and was a symbol of peace when meeting new Indian tribes along the way.

Little is known about Sacajawea until the portage of the Great Falls on the Missouri. She and her baby, along with Captain Clark, nearly drowned in a flash flood after a severe thunderstorm and soon after became very ill. She was near death when the group found a hot spring and possibly the sulfur in the water helped her overcome the sickness.

FINDING THE SHOSHONE INDIANS

When the expedition arrived at the Beaverhead River, Sacajawea remembered the countryside and knew they were near her people. About fifteen miles north and west of Dillon, Montana, they found her brother Cameahwait and his tribe. Three days were spent trading and feasting with the Shoshone. More maps were drawn on skins. Here the boats were left behind and supplies transferred to horses. Sacajawea continued on with the expedition and was again helpful when they met the Nez Perce Indians on the Clearwater River in Idaho.

SYMBOL OF FRIENDSHIP

Sacajawea's presence with her baby Pompy, served as a symbol of friendship whenever they encountered new tribes along the way. No one knows just how helpful she was toward the success of the two-year journey, but it was certain her ability to communicate with the different tribes was a major contribution. This enabled Lewis and Clark to share trade goods such as beads, knives, guns, mirrors, and other things with the Indian tribes they met.

During the next twenty to thirty years, the goodwill spread by Lewis and Clark helped the Americans deal with the Mandan, Sioux, Crow, Shoshone, and other tribes. The Blackfeet Indians of northwestern Montana, however, considered Americans as their enemies for nearly fifty years.

The Sacajawea Hotel, Bed & Breakfast, in Three Forks, Montana, illustrates one of the many establishments using the Indian woman's name.

POMPEY'S PILLAR

On the return east, Captain Clark took a different route and arranged to meet Captain Lewis at the mouth of the Yellowstone River. Lewis took the northern route to study the Marias River. Captain Clark traveled over land to the Yellowstone River and camped near a large sandstone rock formation, on which he carved his name. He called the rock formation Pompy's Rock after Sacajawea's son. Pompy means first-born. Since then the name has been changed to Pompey's Pillar.

From this point, Sergeant Pryor and several men were dispatched to ride south and then east to explore the area. The first night they camped near mountains some twenty miles south. During the night the Crow Indians stole all the horses, leaving the men no choice but to return and continue on with Captain Clark. Sergeant Pryor left his mark, however, as the Pryor Mountains where they camped are named after him.

Most of the history of the expedition, including the time that Sacajawea accompanied them, is found in the journals. Sacajawea and Charbonneau left the expedition when they returned to the Mandan villages. However, the romance of her name and her participation in this famous trip, made her a mystical figure whose memory has grown larger than life.

THE THREE FORKS OF THE MISSOURI

This region was alive with beaver, otter and game before the white man came. It was disputed hunting territory with the Indian tribes. Sacajawea, the Shoshone squaw who guided portions of the Lewis and Clark Expedition, was captured near here when a child, during a battle between her people and the Minnetarees. Her memories of this country were invaluable to the explorers. The Expedition, westward bound, encamped near here for a few days in the latter part of July, 1805. The following year Captain Clark and party came back, July 13, 1806, on their way to explore the Yellowstone River.

In 1808 John Colter, discoverer of Yellowstone Park, and former member of the Lewis and Clark Expedition, was trapping on a stream in this vicinity when captured by a band of Blackfeet. His only companion was killed. Colter was stripped, given a head start, and ordered to run across the flat which was covered with prickly pear. The Indians were hot on his heels but Colter undoubtedly made an all time record that day for sprints as well as distance events. He outran the Indians over a six-mile course and gained the cover of the timber along the Jefferson River. Once in the stream he dove and came up under a jam of driftwood. This hide-out saved him from a lot of disappointed and mystified Indians. When night came he headed east, weaponless and outnuding the nudists. He traveled in this condition for seven days to Fort Lisa, his headquarters, at the mouth of the Big Horn River.

In 1810 the Missouri Fur Co. built a fur trading post close by but due to the hostility of the Blackfeet Indians were forced to abandon it that fall.

One of the brass plates in honor of Sacajawea.

The Pryor Mountains, located about 40 miles south of Billings, Montana, were named after Nathaniel Pryor. Nathaniel Pryor was part of the Lewis and Clark Expedition that was sent south to explore while Captain Clark was camped along the Yellowstone in 1806. He and several men were to travel east to the Mandan villages. The Crow Indians stole all their horses the first night and they returned unsuccessful to Captain Clark.

THE HORSE

The first horses arrived from Spain in 1519. When the ten stallions and six mares were unloaded from the Spanish galleon, the awesome animal appeared as a spirit to the Native Americans. The Indians called the horse Elk Dog, Medicine Dog, or God Dog. Within several hundred years, the Indians as far north as Canada acquired the horse.

The buffalo was used for food, clothing, shelter, and considered a gift from the gods to the Indians. However, the horse brought mobility and was a companion, packer, and warrior. More than any other single event, the horse changed forever the life of the Indian. They could hunt more efficiently, enabling them to expand their territories and gather more food, increasing the Indian population.

Ownership of horses created a better lifestyle and were a prize worth stealing from other tribes. Horses were accepted by the father for the hand of his maiden daughter in marriage. A brave's wealth was often measured by the number of horses in his corral. Revered by the Indians, the horses were painted and decorated with feathers.

An Indian brave on his horse, armed with bow and arrow or spear, was a formidable opponent in combat. On the smaller, stronger, and more durable mustang, they out rode the larger horses ridden by the cavalry. The soldiers' expertise never equaled the horsemanship of the Indians.

The horse gave the Indians the ability to travel hundreds of miles from central North Dakota to southwest Montana, and into New Mexico and California. Within hours, an Indian woman could pull camp, putting all the belongings on a travois pulled by a horse. The Plains Indian lifestyle focused on travel. They used the horse to follow game herds, move to milder areas during harsh winters, and to do faraway trading.

THE COWBOY

Later, the cowboy of the west found the horse a welcome comrade. Cattle could ramble through the roughest land and nothing was better than a good range-bred horse to wrangle cows out of the scab canyons. Teams of horses pulled plows, wagons, and stagecoaches for the early settlers, making the west a better place to live. For several hundred years, the horse was the primary source of power, and horsepower still remains the basic measure of energy.

The Appaloosa horses of early European breeding were brought to America by the Spaniards. The Appaloosa horse was well formed, intelligent, and generally black or gray. Characteristic spots, especially on the rump, were particularly attractive to the Indians. The Nez Perce Indians of the Wallowa country came to own these horses and in the beautiful rich, grassy flats stretching for miles, the Appaloosa horse flourished under their stewardship. The Nez Perce began careful breeding by selection for disposition, intelligence, color, size, and trainability. The horses were used for hunting, raiding, work, and racing. They taught the horse to respond to

The Appaloosa horse bred by the Nez Perce Indians with the characteristic spotted rump, is considered a top western breed, today.

knee pressure commands, leaving their hands free to shoot a bow and arrow. The horses were trained to stop, stay put when the Indian warrior dismounted, and come when signaled. In concert, the Indian and his horse were superior to the army or cavalry soldier. During the Nez Perce March, their ability in hit-and-run warfare made a mockery of the American generals.

One of the sad chapters in American history occurred after the surrender of Chief Joseph in the Bearpaw Mountains. Concluding that these Appaloosa horses made the Indians such great warriors, the army confiscated their horses. The horses were driven into a ravine and shot.

Beartooth Batholith

The upthrust of this mass of granite illustrates how the geological happenings occurred in the Rocky Mountains. The average height is 11,000 feet with 29 peaks reaching 12,000 feet above sea level.

The geological changes of the rising of the Rocky Mountains created new geography and the Missouri River Country.

Shallow seas disappeared and became swamps, then gradually changed to evergreen forests, grasslands and deserts. Animals, like dinosaurs, needing great volumes of food became extinct, while smaller mammals (deer, elk, buffalo) adapted to a grass diet. Carnivores, like Sabertooth Tigers, gradually mutated to bobcats, cougars, or became history.

Geology dictates geography and geography dictates plant and animal habitat. Humans react to the available resources.

CHAPTER 3
The Missouri River Country Geology

Missouri River Geology

The early geology of the Missouri River Country was a series of shallow seas stretching from the Arctic Ocean to the Gulf of Mexico. These inland sea periods were from 600 to 225 million years ago (Paleozoic) and 225 to 60 million years ago (Mesozoic).

The Paleozoic Period is made up of Cambrian, Ordovician, Silurian, Devonian, Mississippian, Pennsylvanian, and Permian periods of time. During the eras of Paleozoic and Mesozoic, layer upon layer of sediment, plant growth, and skeletons of tiny sea creatures were forming strata across the broad flats of North America. These layers can be seen exposed in the Rocky Mountains today. The Mesozoic Era consisted of three periods: Triassic, Jurassic, and Cretaceous, the time frames when life accelerated on earth and the dinosaurs roamed.

Shallow seas of the Ordovician, Silurian, Devonian, Mississippian, and Pennsylvanian periods were ideal for small brachiopods and other creatures. Their skeletons created layer upon layer of limestone. After faulting, exposures of these 400 million year old rock formations were exposed in the Rocky Mountain system of the Missouri River Country.

ERA	PERIOD	EPOCH	AGE MIL YEARS	EARTH'S AGE CHART
Cenozoic Age of Mammals	Quaternary	Holocene	1/100	
		Pliestocene	2	
	Tertiary	Pilocene	3	
		Miocene	24	
		Ikugicebe	37	
		Eocene	58	
		Paleocene	66	
Mesozoic Age of Reptiles	Cretaceous		144	
	Jurassic		208	
	Triassic		245	
Paleozoic Age of Fishes	Triassic		286	
	Pennsylvanian		320	
	Mississippian		360	
	Devonian		408	
	Silurian		438	
	Ordovician		505	
	Cambrian		570	
Protozoic Pre-Cambrian	Younger		2500	
	Older		4700	

The Earth's Age Chart helps explain how we think events evolved from 4.7 billion years ago up to the present time. During the late Cretaceous and early Tertiary periods, the mountains began forming and this event changed swamps to forest, deserts, and life on this part of Earth. In several places along the east slopes of the Rocky Mountains, the earliest plant life fossils are found, and also in the Beartooths, Pryors, and Bighorns, fossils of Ordovician, Devonian, and Mississippian periods are found.

39

THE EARTH'S STRUCTURE

The earth is thought to have a core in the center, an intermediate area called a mantle, and a thin outer area called a crust or lithosphere. The mantle consists of molten rock materials, moving slowly. The outer layer is a series of plates fitting together similar to a jigsaw puzzle. The outer crust floats over the hot molten mantle, and the very inner core is thought to be nickel and iron. The molten mantle is under immense pressure and if any cracks in the outer surface occur, molten magma rises to the surface forming volcanoes which spew out new igneous materials that eventually cool and reshape the outer surface of the earth. If sedimentary layers are buried deep, heat and pressure change these materials into metamorphic rock. Sedimentary rock is usually soft material, such as sandstone, limestone, and mud shale.

Sometime during the late Cretaceous Period, mountain orogeny (mountain building) began. During this time the Atlantic sea floor began to open, pushing westward the Continental Plate. Meanwhile a similar happening in the Pacific Ocean caused the Pacific Plate to move toward the center of North America. At the point of contact, a fracturing of the lithosphere occurred. This created the volcanic activity of the Cascade Mountains along the Pacific shoreline. As the volcanic materials poured out, the lands called Oregon and Washington were formed.

The compression caused by the plates moving toward each other - the Pacific Plate moving eastward and the Continental Plate moving westward - happened between 70 and 60 millions years ago. During this movement and the fracturing of the lithosphere, the Rocky Mountains began to form. Large granite

The Earth's Interior Structure

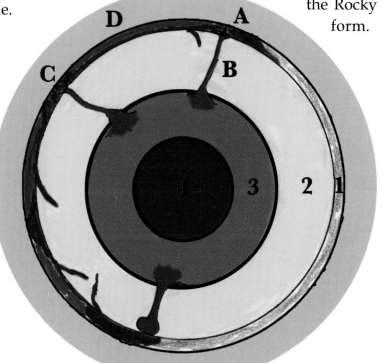

1. *Lithosphere - 4 Mi. to 40 Mi. thick*
2. *Mantle - 1800 Mi.*
3. *Outer Core - 1400 Mi.*
4. *Inner Core - 1540 Miles, 3700 deg. F.*
5. *A = Yellowstone Park*
6. *B = Plume of molten materials*
7. *C = Hawaiian Islands*
8. *D = Oceans*

The lithosphere is a restless crust on top of the mantle fitting much like a jigsaw puzzle. The mantle is semi-molten and moving in slow currents. The material is more dense than crustal rock. The core is thought to be heavy materials of nickel and iron and here, intense pressures keep the center solid.

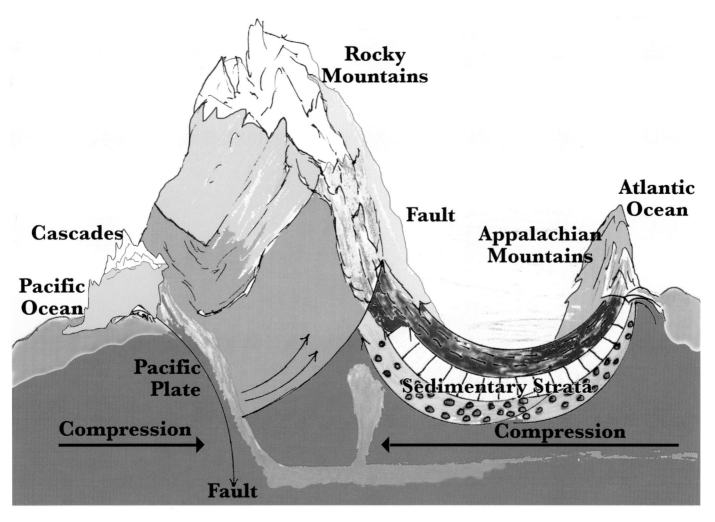

The compression of the lithosphere, or crust, may have shortened the distance between the Atlantic Ocean and Pacific Ocean by nearly 400 miles.

intrusions were forced upward, creating what is known as batholiths. These actions caused the uplifting of sedimentary strata and the sliding of these plates eastward created stacking, folding, and faulting. The largest was the Beartooth batholith. This also happened in southwestern Montana and eastern Idaho, and these batholiths are named the Idaho, Boulder, and the Bitterroot.

During this time, entire areas of sedimentary rock strata slid eastward fifty or sixty miles. The movement probably occurred on top of water-soaked clay areas which served as skids for the large strata to move. This fracturing and uplifting of batholiths, sliding of plates, and volcanic eruptions created the majestic Rocky Mountains. The Rocky Mountains stretch from Alaska to Central America. The study of the Rocky Mountain formation is complicated because many of these geologic events occurred in the same areas. While the Idaho batholith was breaking up and sliding, the lithosphere was also fracturing near Yellowstone Park in southwestern Montana. The Absaroka volcanoes occurred about 50 million years ago, pouring out cubic miles of cinder, ash, and lava. Intermingled with this action was the uplifting of sedimentary strata and the uplifting caused faulting and created violent earthquakes. In some places the sea floor was thrust several miles upward.

Geologists give names to the origin of rocks.

Sandstone Rock

• *Sandstone is formed as materials are washed into lakes and oceans leaving sediment. Over the years it hardens but is still considered soft rock.*

• *Metamorphic rock is sedimentary rock transformed under heat and pressure to hard rock-like marble.*

• *Igneous rock is molten material forced out of the Earth's mantle as granite and lava.*

Metamorphic Rock

Intrusive Igneous Rock

The upthrusts and compression created mountain areas looking like stacked blocks.

Some of the earthquake faults are still active in the Yellowstone Park area which remains the largest hot spot in North America. The Rocky Mountains area from Helena, Montana to the Canadian border was formed by faulting and upthrusting although some volcanic activity also happened. The smashing of the plates against each other caused the Pacific Plate to slide under the Continental Plate, but this action was not uniform and many small mountain units were formed along the Rocky Mountain chain. Early visitors to this crumpled land gave these smaller mountains such names as Bighorn, Pryor, Tobacco Root, Gravelly, Bearpaw, Little Belt, and Big Belt.

The Yellowstone Park hot spot has created 10,000 hot springs and geysers, all producing mineralized waters for trout streams.

The names reflected the character of the mountains but sometimes were named after the men who first saw them.

Some of these mountains were formed during the early Tertiary times and in the Belt Mountains, volcanoes produced radial dikes which radiate out much like spines on a fish's back. These Shonkinite lavas flowed from an eruptive source similar to spokes on a wheel, leaving dome-shaped laccoliths at the ends. These can be seen near Cascade, Montana and at the northern end of the Highwood Mountain volcanics. Other volcanic happenings created diatremes. These igneous intrusions often produced sapphires, the most famous being the

43

blue Yogo sapphire. These crystals were formed as igneous intrusions cooled.

The Tertiary Period ended 2.5 million years ago and the Quaternary Period is from then to present time. During the Quaternary Period, the Yellowstone Park volcanoes have erupted three times. The first was two million years ago pushing out 600 cubic miles of material. The second was 1.6 million years ago pushing out 67 cubic miles of material and the third was 600,000 years ago pushing out 240 cubic miles of material. This movement of lava, ash, and cinder, thought to total 907 cubic miles, were the world's largest ever volcanic eruptions. They caused major changes in the topography of the surrounding areas of the Missouri River country and added to the constant erosion of the Missouri River system. Even today, this ash continues to erode into the river system after each hard rain.

THE GLACIAL AGES

The glacial Ice Age followed these eruptions: 130,000 years ago, 70,000 years ago, and 15,000 years ago. Again, these events profoundly affected the topography of the Missouri River

Basalt lavas are more familiar and look like giant five-sided hanging crystals.

country. The Bull Lake Ice Age created large glacial lakes: Great Falls Lake, Musselshell Lake, and Lake Glendive. Geologists believe that at one time, it was possible to boat from Cut Bank, Montana to Glendive, Montana during the glacial lake era - a distance over 700 miles.

The glaciers helped flatten the land of northern Montana and northern North Dakota and changed the course of the Missouri River several times. The melting ice cap left numerous boulders scattered erratically across the land. The glaciers also affected the pile up

The Shonkinite Lavas of the Belt Mountains radiate out and, in some areas, diatremes form with sapphire crystals. The Yogo deep blue gems are the best known of the Missouri River stones.

The glacial lake, Great Falls, covered much of northern Montana east of the Rocky Mountains. During its time, sediments were washed in by the Missouri River. When the lake finally drained, excellent farm land was left stretching from sunrise to sunset.

of cinder, ash, and other materials allowing streams to shape the Badlands. These unusual landscapes created by erosion formed in and around the Missouri Breaks, the Glendive area at Makoshika Park, and throughout the Little Missouri River system, especially at Theodore Roosevelt National Park.

The Rocky Mountains are many things: wild, beautiful, rugged. Giving life to the plains both east and west, they are a treasure and should be respected.

FORMING THE MISSOURI RIVER

The mountains are a symbol of creation stretching high into the sky exposing their craggy tops to every natural happening. Time, countless raindrops, and snowflakes chip away at their faces. The surfaces freeze, warm up, then freeze again, and with each temperature change continual expansion and contraction occurs. This action causes the faces of mountains to undergo constant erosion.

The Missouri River system depends on the Rocky Mountains to extract moisture from the air currents circling the earth. The currents move upward and over the mountains, causing cooling and the formation of precipitation, falling sometimes as rain and sometimes as snow. The water feeds small streams which grow into creeks which flow into rivers - into the Missouri, then into the Mississippi, and finally to the Gulf of Mexico. This relay system takes place all over the world and allows life to thrive on planet Earth.

The upper Missouri River drainage is very large. Two thirds of Montana, sixty percent of Wyoming, some of Canada, western North Dakota, South Dakota, and parts of Nebraska waters flow into this river system. The semi-arid countryside is subject to drought and floods which explains why the river is called the wild and muddy Missouri. Geologically, the drainage is young, and massive erosion has always been a factor. After the mountain building, the geology during the Tertiary Period was generally quiet. Some small mountain ranges were formed by volcanic activity in the Eocene Epoch but in general, erosion and glaciers caused the major changes in the Missouri River country.

The Gallatin River flows out of the Gallatin Mountains in the northwest corner of Yellowstone Park. Here the river begins gathering small streams to travel down and out of the mountains. The river is joined by the East Gallatin flowing out of the Bridgers and continues westward to meet the Missouri River at Three Forks, Montana. The Madison River drains the northwestern side of Yellowstone and the Madison Mountain Range. The Madison leaves Yellowstone Park near West Yellowstone and flows north to meet the Jefferson River at Three Forks, Montana. The Jefferson is formed by the Ruby River, the Beaverhead and the Big Hole rivers. The Jefferson, Madison, and Gallatin rivers meet to form the Missouri River at Three Forks, Montana. Here, at the confluence of these three rivers, the first white Americans, Lewis and Clark, camped in August of 1805.

The Rocky Mountains steal moisture from the westerly flowing winds and create our weather and geography. The winter storms leave snow and this moisture, when evaporating in the summer, starts the thundershower activity.

THE ROCKY MOUNTAINS CREATE THE MISSOURI RIVER CLIMATE

The weather of the Missouri River Country is as varied as anywhere in the world.

The mountains claim moisture from the prevailing westerly winds circling the earth in the temperate zone. In winter, Arctic cold air masses slide down from Alaska and Canada and these cold fronts often meet Pacific warm fronts to create winter storms.

Spring cyclonic air masses working counterclockwise up from the Gulf of Mexico bring rains as they stall against the mountains. Summertime, as the sun warms this area of America, rising convection currents create thunder storms that ramble eastward toward the midwest. These weather systems travel in a southeasterly manner from their origination high in the Rockies.

This Missouri River country is a definite four-season climate for the Missouri River Country with temperature varying from 100 degrees in the summer to -30 degrees in the winter. These extremes don't stay long and the mean temperature is usually very agreeable.

Some areas, Billings, Great Falls, Helena, Choteau, receive descending winds called chinooks, keeping winter snows melted away allowing a milder climate for the latitude than other parts of the world.

In general, the climates throughout the areas from northern Wyoming to the Montana hi-line, western North Dakota and South Dakota are easy living.

Winter snows quickly melt and summer temperatures are mostly in the high 80's.

Sunny days number around 300 annually and rainfall ranges from 7 to 25 inches scattered throughout the year. Wind influences some areas much more than others especially where air flows off the mountains and is funneled into certain river valleys. Low humidity and lots of sunshine provides pleasant seasons and a very productive work atmosphere.

The Jefferson River Country during the spring and early summer resembles a giant golf course and the beauty is charismatic.

Descending winds flowing down from the mountains create deserts. The Red Canyon, Lander, Wyoming.

The Missouri River Country is a four-season climate with some extremes, but generally pleasant and comfortable.

The dry climate makes summertime fun for all types of outdoor recreation.

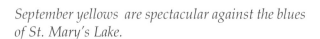
September yellows are spectacular against the blues of St. Mary's Lake.

STUDY THE GEOLOGY OF THE MISSOURI RIVER COUNTRY BY FOSSIL HUNTING

Today, hunting dinosaur and other fossils is a full-time business in the Missouri River Country. Places like Hell's Creek Canyon, Jordan, Montana; Thermopolis, Wyoming; Choteau, Montana, are current digs for these prehistoric animals of the Mesozoic Era.

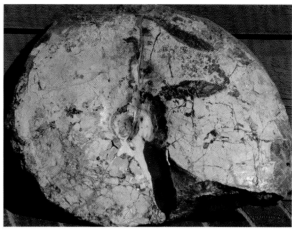

Gastropod fossil found along the lower Musselshell River.

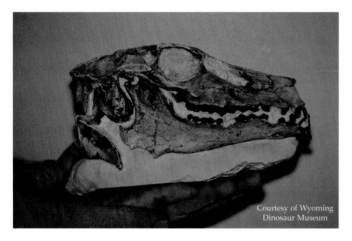

Extinct fossil of pre-historic camel found near Thermopolis, Wyoming.

Tyranosaurus Rex skull found in Hell's Creek Canyon, Jordan, Montana.

The Gold Rush Days of the 1860's

The rising of the Rockies formed new geography and created the Missouri River System. When Lewis and Clark arrived they only visualized a small portion of the resources and how important this new region would become to the United States as a country.

After the expedition, fur traders and trappers began to filter in to every stream throughout the Rocky Mountains. Even though they took the animal skins, they left the countryside untouched. But, in 1862 gold was found and the beautiful countryside began to feel the effects of the White Americans. After gold, the mining shifted to silver, copper, lead, and limestone.

Gold bearing quartz veins run all through the Tobacco Root Mountains near Virginia City.

CHAPTER 4
The Exploitation of the Missouri River Resources

GOLD, OUTLAWS, AND VIGILANTES

Bannack, Montana Territory, now a state park, was the first territorial capital, and flourished as long as gold was produced along Grasshopper Creek.

After the 1804-1806 Lewis and Clark Expedition came the American Fur Company.

Trappers John Colter and later Jim Bridger walked over most of the Rocky Mountains, following every riverlet, taking beaver. Later, these men served as scouts for wagon trains and the military.

1807 to 1840 was the fur exploitation era of the region. After 1840, when beaver hats were no longer the style in Europe, much of the territory was not visited until Jedediah Smith found the South Pass which became the Oregon Trail. From 1847 to 1860, thousands of settlers traveled west hoping for new lives, but still the Montana Territory was left vacant. This was called "Indian Country," and considered of little value.

The Sutters Mill gold strike in California in 1849 brought thousands of men looking for quick wealth, and as one field played out, these miners spread out looking for another nugget.

GRASSHOPPER CREEK IN MIDSUMMER, 1862, JOHN WHITE AND PARTY DISCOVERED GOLD ON THIS CREEK SEVERAL MILES DOWN STREAM. THE FIRST MAJOR GOLD RUSH TO WHAT IS NOW MONTANA RESULTED.

Sign at Bannack State Park.

When flakes of gold showed "pan"-demonium raged up and down the wilderness stream.

Finding gold in the beautiful stream bed of Grasshopper Creek started a completely new era for this desolate and lonesome Indian country called Montana.

GOLD...GOLD...*GOLD*!

Shouts of "GOLD!" echoed across the grass prairies and mountains like thunder after bolts of bright lightning.

In 1862 the first gold strike at Grasshopper Creek was found on a big flat 15 to 20 miles south and west of the town now called Dillon, Montana. Gold was found at Virginia City, Nevada City, Immigrant Creek, Last Chance Gulch, Gold Creek, the Judith Mountains, and the Little Rockies. Like ants, miners grubbed, scratched, and placered millions of dollars of the yellow metal from the mountainsides and stream beds.

TO THE INDIANS IT SEEMED LIKE "HELL ON EARTH!"

The fever was so bad, it spawned a town located miles from Salt Lake City, Denver, San Francisco, or any other place which might be considered civilized. As one old-timer noted, "This country is so lonesome, an eagle would

have trouble finding a mate." This first town Bannack, Montana Territory, mushroomed overnight and during the next twenty years, $16,000,000 in gold was dug and sluiced from the gravel and hillsides along beautiful Grasshopper Creek. Now a celebrated ghost town, Bannack gave birth to tales of Sheriff Henry Plummer, Mary Wadams, and a cayuse horse named Ives. Here began the first capital, first church, first school, first Masonic Hall, to name just a few. In its heyday, the town boasted three hundred people but at times many more lived in tents scattered along the creek. The territorial capital was moved to Virginia City, a larger and more active mining town several years later. After statehood, however, the capital was moved to Helena and Bannack was left to be reclaimed by nature. Still, there remains the legacy of a young boy's dream envisioning himself outdrawing Henry Plummer or one of his outlaw buddies, Stinson, Ray, or George Ives on a dusty, western street.

HENRY PLUMMER

Law and order became the topic of the day, as the collection of men in this new town were a bag full of scruffs no one would want. They came from Colorado, Missouri, California, and who knows where. Upon this scene rode a well-dressed man of eastern vintage, Henry Plummer, whose manners and conversation won him the friendship of storekeepers and other city fathers. Even the women of Bannack, who were mostly followers from one gold camp to another, took a liking to Henry.

Henry decided he needed to marry to improve his image; he courted and "won the hand" of Electra Bryan. This opened the door for Henry to build a highly respectable image and run for sheriff, while his gang, the "Innocents" plundered.

The first Sheriff, Hank Crawford, departed on a steamboat out of Fort Benton to escape Plummer's gun. It took Electra fewer than three months to decide this marriage was bad, climb on a stage to Salt Lake City, never to return. The townspeople, however, didn't see the picture.

Sheriff Henry Plummer and his gang robbed stages running from Salt Lake City to Bannack, or from Bannack to Virginia City, or from Bannack to Helena. When considering the $16 million in gold dug in Bannack, $23 million placered near Virginia City, and multiples of this amount from Deer Lodge and Last Chance Gulch, robbing stagecoaches, travelers, and freighters proved to be a very lucrative business, especially when shielded by the "star." Plummer's connections and ability to comfortably mingle with bankers, storekeepers and others in the know, gave the sheriff inside knowledge as to when and how the gold was being shipped.

Courtesy of Hall

Sheriff Henry Plummer's gang, called "The Innocents," robbed stages, individuals, freighters, and killed if it was expedient.

Henry would wave goodbye to the stage and its passengers. He and his gang would then ride hard ahead, stop the stage out of town to rob and even kill if necessary. Henry would meet the stage at the next town down the line where he would be "utterly amazed" and would swear to "git those ruffians soon." One plucky passenger, Henry Tilden, recognized Plummer's horse during a holdup and this discovery led to formation of the Vigilantes.

Henry Plummer and two of his gang members, Stinson and Ray, were the first three "hung by the neck 'til dead" and were left, frozen and swinging, for everyone to see as the sun lit the gruesome scene the next morning. Soon thereafter Joe Pizanthia, known as "Greaser", met the same fate and then George Ives was swinging next. After the swift action of the Vigilantes, the Montana Territory became a safer place to live and the remaining outlaws quickly looked for new country.

The Bannack Jail...while Henry Plummer was sheriff, you were safer in jail than out!

Ten miles east of Bannack on the old route to Virginia City still stands the first stage stop where worn and tired horses were replaced with fresh horses.

Virginia City

Gold was found just over the hill in Alder Gulch shortly after the Grasshopper Creek strike.

Virginia City was thrown up much like a western movie set. "Quick and dirty," said one old miner; "and enough to get out of the rain for a whiskey."

Between the Tobacco Root and Gravelly mountains, gold bearing quartz lodes cropped out of the countryside. Montana history bloomed with placer, dredges, and hard rock mines. Small towns like Virginia City, Adobetown, and Nevada City were built almost overnight. These frontier towns were largely bars, dance halls, gambling joints, and supply stores for the miners. Between 1863 and into the 1880's, the Saturday night ruckus could be heard for miles...until the gold played out.

The territorial capital was moved from Bannack to Virginia city, and later the area was served by the Union Pacific Railroad.

Gold is as fickle as clouds swirling over a high mountain peak and the mining in the Montana Territory was here one day...gone the next.

Downtown Virginia City late 1990's.

During the Gold Fever Days of the Montana Territory over in the Snake River country of the Wallowa Mountains, the U.S. Military was attempting to force the Nez Perce Indians to leave their home land and move to a reservation out in the desert. Nez Perce resistance led to the retreat to Canada across Idaho and Montana through the area of Bannack, Montana Territory.

courtesy of Blaine County Museum

The newspaper press portrayed Chief Joseph a great American hero.

THE INDIAN HISTORY
CHIEF JOSEPH OF THE NEZ PERCE

The Nez Perce Indians occupied the Idaho lands on the lower Clearwater to the Salmon River and across the Snake into the Wallowa Country of eastern Oregon. These Indian lands of Oregon and Idaho were rich in game. Elk, deer, antelope, and salmon from the Pacific Ocean were abundant, and once a year the tribes moved eastward to hunt buffalo in the southwestern Montana Territory. They also supplemented their diet with roots and berries, which gave these people the foundation for an expanding culture.

The Nez Perce Indians were stately, tall, with good features and well-mannered. They were known to be generally peaceful with the White Americans. In all, the Nez Perce Indians were considered exemplary of how an Indian nation would be viewed. They selectively bred their horses, developing a special breed called the Appaloosa. This horse was very intelligent, fast, and durable. With his horse, the Nez Perce warrior was considered a great fighter and feared by the American military.

THE NEZ PERCE MARCH

The story of Chief Joseph's famed Nez Perce March started in the Wallowa Mountains of eastern Oregon. General Henry Ottis Howard, using an unsigned treaty, was ordering the Nez Perce Indians on to reservations and allowing white settlers, miners, and ranchers to move onto Indian lands. During this parley, a young brave decided to avenge his father's death, who was killed for no apparent reason by a white man named Henry Ott. He and other young Indian braves killed several whites who had been mistreating the Indians.

General Howard quickly seized this opportunity to exert military authority and make a show of leadership by marching on the Nez Perce. Also, under his command, Howard sent Captain Perry to force the Indians off these lands and on to a reservation. His intent was to destroy this unruly band of Indians.

The Indian women, in their skin boats, could move across the Snake River with ease while the U.S. Military often lost half of their supplies in their clumsy, make-shift boats.

Boise, Walla Walla, Burns and outfitted with cannons and the new rapid-fire Gatling guns. However, the military in all its glory with bugles, flags, freight wagons, cannons, and Gatling guns were clumsy travelers in a country with rough, steep canyons. The Indians could make fools of them. The Indian women, with their skin boats, could cross the rivers more easily than the Army, and the war chiefs quickly learned to use hit-and-run warfare.

GENERAL HOWARD'S CONTINUED PROBLEMS

The Indians knew they would die of starvation on the reservations as wards of the United States government. They decided to fight and hid in the grassy ravines, waiting for Captain Perry to come to them. In one fierce battle the Indians nearly exterminated Perry and his soldiers, killing 38 and wounding that many more. One Indian was slightly injured, thus General Howard realized this small band of Nez Perce Indians were better schooled at warfare than his career military soldiers. The Appaloosa horses were fast and well trained and at full gallop, the braves could shoot arrows with deadly accuracy from under the necks of their horses - a practice learned from childhood while hunting game.

Chief Joseph and his war chiefs yearned for peace but after their humiliating victory over Captain Perry, General Howard was determined to pursue and destroy the Indians. There seemed no choice for them but to begin the retreat across the Snake River and in to Canada. The cavalry and armies were now coming from several directions -

General Howard was chronicled in American papers as an inept leader unable to whip a small band of Indians retreating with squaws and children. After several scrimmages, the Indians had lost but one brave while the army suffered significant numbers of dead and wounded. The Army was portrayed as having no chance of cornering Chief Joseph's people while herding 2,500 horses through the mountains. The retreat proceeded up the Clearwater toward Lolo Pass and Bitterroot Valley in Montana where once again General Howard walked into an ambush along the river, losing yet more

The Snake River Canyons were rugged and difficult for the U.S. Military.

men. A mere eighteen Indian braves had insulted him, and the papers loved the story.

MONTANA'S BITTERROOT VALLEY

On July 24, 1877, as the Nez Perce reached Lolo Pass to cross into the Bitterroot Valley, the scouts knew the Army was waiting. Captian Rawn had been dispatched to set up a fort and stop the Indians at Lolo Pass, later called Fort Fizzle because the Nez Perce outflanked the Army. Without firing a shot, the Indians told the Army they were going through into the valley, and did so without incident. They traded for or bought the food they needed from white settlers who had been friends with them for years. The settlers were not harmed but the egos of generals had been badly bruised.

The band of Indians were headed up the Bitterroot Valley to cross southern Montana following a route close to the one Lewis and Clark traversed seventy years before. They were joined by a famous hunter, Lean Elk, who became their guide. The whites called him Poker Joe, the son of a French-Canadian. His mother, a Nez Perce Indian. He was needed to guide the Nez Perce into and through the Rocky Mountain area of Yellowstone Park and north to Canada.

Colonel Gibbon was now in the area and eager to engage the Nez Perce. Gibbon managed a sneak attack on the sleeping camp of Indians. They had posted no guards and felt safe since most people in the Montana Territory were friendly. Gibbon's men indiscriminantly killed nearly one hundred women and children. It was still a terrible loss for the Nez Perce. Gibbon and his men were at first regarded as heroes until the real truth surfaced and exposed them as ruthless killers.

THE EFFECT OF GIBBON'S ATTACK

After scattering naked into the rocks, the Nez Perce braves gathered, returned to whip Gibbon, killing 29 soldiers and wounding 40 more. From then on, Chief Joseph could not

contain the anger of young warriors who believed all whites should be annihilated. The Indians pressed on toward Bannack, the first town in the Montana Territory. The settlers and ranchers were hurrying for safety - some did not make it. The young warriors stole cattle, horses, and food as they moved eastward across southern Montana. The now wounded tribe of Indians were taking a route to Yellowstone Park and then into the Crow Country of the Yellowstone River. In years past they hunted with the Crow Indians and Chief Joseph felt they would get help from his friends.

The Nez Perce warrior riding his famed Appaloosa horse made the U.S. Cavalry and soldiers look juvenile, and this was of great delight for the newspapers.

THE FAMOUS MARY WADAMS RIDE

Mary Wadams kept a small buckskin horse in her back yard in Bannack, Montana Territory. Her horse, called Ives, was her great friend. Most folks would not have found much use for a cayuse, meaning Indian horse. Ives was considered an outlaw. Having been mistreated by men trying to ride him, he would go "plum crazy" if a man tried to put a hand on him. But Mary brought Ives oats every morning and soon they were friends. The cayuse was an Indian-bred animal, tough as nails, and able to easily travel over Montana's rough terrain and scabby hills. Most whites preferred a Morgan or Tennessee Walking horse but Mary felt Ives was worth the oats she fed him every day. The little horse trusted no one but her.

Mary had settled in Montana's Beaverhead country in 1862, the first white woman to live in this forlorn, isolated section of the west. Pioneer women either grew strong or withered and died. Mary grew stronger over the years, becoming a great horsewoman, and could shoot a gun as well as most men. Courage was another factor these tough pioneer women developed, and it did not hurt to have wit and perseverance to handle problems.

For no apparent reason, Henry Ott had earlier killed a Nez Perce Indian called Eagle Robe. Eagle Robe's son, along with other young braves, went on the warpath to avenge the death of his father. Ott somehow escaped but other white men who had mistreated the Nez Perce were killed. This incident set off the Nez Perce war and led to the famous Chief Joseph march from Oregon, through Idaho, and into Montana.

The band of Indians thought they had

The mustang horse evolved from Spanish ancestry and ran wild throughout the West. The Indians liked these animals for their toughness and ability to survive the northern winters. Mary Wadams' buckskin horse was of this vintage.

escaped General Howard and were camped near the Big Hole River, unaware of General Gibbon's presence in the area. During the night of August 8, Colonel Gibbon pulled a sneak attack on the sleeping Indian village, killing 53 women and 39 children. Until this time, the Nez Perce had simply ignored the whites traveling through the Bitterroot Valley, but now they considered all whites as an enemy to be killed. Chief Joseph was leading his band of Nez Perce Indians to Canada, but after the mass killing of women and children by Gibbon, he could no longer control the anger of his young braves.

Small war parties spread out across Horse Prairie burning, looting, and stealing horses. Cattlemen rode ahead, carrying the bad news from ranch to ranch. The whites were quickly heading for Bannack to barricade the town from the expected Indian attack. Fear ruled in Bannack, barricades were built, food was stashed in the safest place with the women and children at the back of the buildings.

Mary's two sons Dick, seventeen and Duncan, eleven, had taken jobs as cowboys with a cattle company on Horse Prairie, about seventy-five miles from Bannack. The boys were tending cattle and camp chores, oblivious to the Indian uprising around them.

NO HELP GIVEN

Mary Wadams found herself in a dilemma - should she rescue her sons alone or ask for help. Mary asked the men if they would ride with her to warn her sons. The men refused, saying they were sorry but felt it was too risky to travel into warring Indian country. Mary said, "I will go it alone." She saddled little Ives and headed out to Horse Prairie, armed with only an umbrella. On a hot, August day Mary rode the little cayuse seventy-five miles across the countryside. The umbrella saved her from sunstroke and she rested Ives whenever he needed to stop. During the day the buckskin color of the horse faded into the dry, grassy

hillsides. Mary avoided the ridge lines, preferring to travel just under the tops of the hills. She rode right into the face of her oldest son, Dick, who had left Duncan alone in camp in order to head to Bannack for tobacco. Returning to camp with his mother, Dick rode out to report the Indian uprising to the other cowmen while Mary remained in camp with Duncan and rested. The three made the 75-mile return trip to Bannack in thirteen hours. The welcome party was out and the 150-mile ride made on a little old Indian horse named Ives is recorded as a legend.

Mary Wadams died in Dillon, Montana in 1921 at the age of 91 years and 249 days. She was truly one of the old pioneer stock conquering the West.

The Nez Perce traveled several miles west of Bannack enroute to Yellowstone Park leaving the white population without conflict.

YELLOWSTONE NATIONAL PARK

On their trail, General Howard became more determined than ever to wipe out the Indians. In his haste he was depleting his supplies and wearing down his horses. His men began complaining and the newspapers and Army were more critical. There was talk of replacing him as bickering between the soldiers and volunteers continued.

Armies and cavalries were approaching from all directions to surround the marching band of squaws, children, and horses. Again, the

The Nez Perce Indians on their travels not only had to avoid the military, they needed to traverse a very difficult and rugged terrain. Eagle Robe, famous hunter, was to lead the Nez Perce around the Yellowstone Canyon enroute out of the park to Canada.

ambush. Then while the military slept under Howard's watch, forty braves marched in columns of four into their camp at Camas Meadows, and stole most of the horses and mules. This crippled General Howard again, and he became the laughing stock of America. Whipped and ridiculed, he became increasingly frustrated.

THE TRAP WAS SET AT ALL CORNERS OF YELLOWSTONE PARK

The Indians kept the generals guessing by taking routes the military could not follow, foiling any attempts at ambush. Lieutenant Doane's unit was stationed where the Yellowstone River flowed out of the mountains, now called Livingston, Montana. Colonel Sturgis was camped at the mouth of canyon of the Clark's Fork River. Major Hart stood guard at Cody where the Shoshone River flowed out of the Absaroka Mountains. General Howard was coming from behind. The military felt certain they had the fox in a box as the Indians could not travel out of Yellowstone Park without battle on the military terms.

Though tired, worn, and becoming desperate themselves, the Indians were still out maneuvering the armies and the American press were making a joke out of this circus. In Yellowstone Park some white visitors were captured by the Nez Perce. The women were released unharmed and told the press of the statesmanship of Chief Joseph. This news echoed across the United States as yet more stories were written. While in Yellowstone Park, the Indians captured a prospector, John Shivel, who guided the band through the toughest terrain of the park. The press continued to stretch the stories like "a man's neck hanging from a tree."

THE AMERICAN PUBLIC WAS BECOMING SYMPATHETIC TOWARD THE INDIANS

The band traveled a route northeast over the Absaroka Mountains into the Clark's Fork Canyon. From there, they decided to travel over Dead Indian Pass and walked right by Colonel Sturgis. The Army had stumbled once again. White America was becoming sympathetic, and hoping the Indians could make it to Canada. The band traversed the Clark's Fork River to the Yellowstone River near Billings, Montana. Their travel route took them up Canyon Creek then over the divide into the Musselshell River crossing near the town of Ryegate, Montana. They turned west when hounded by Sturgis, and headed through Judith Gap crossing the Missouri at Cow Island. Located there was a small Army post guarding riverboat shipments of supplies. The four civilians and a dozen soldiers guarding the cache were no match for the Nez Perce. The Indians quickly overran the fort, taking flour, beans, and other supplies. War Chief Yellow Wolf said this was Indian play.

THE BEARPAW MOUNTAINS

The tribe continued on to the Bearpaw Mountains and camped 42 miles from the Canadian border. Chief Joseph wanted to push on to the border but the war chiefs, under Chief Looking Glass, overruled and decided to stay and rest before continuing on to Canada. Freedom was only a few steps away. This fateful mistake allowed General Miles, coming from Fort Keogh near Miles City, to catch them. Here he attacked the Indians camped in a ravine. The Indians quickly grouped and nearly wiped out General Miles and his brigade, but Chief Joseph was unaware of how close to defeat was Miles' Army. General Miles pulled back to organize a siege. The Indians were now cold, hungry, and in trouble. Some stole away into the night to continue on to Canada. General Miles sent a message to Chief Joseph that Howard and Sturgis were near and urged their surrender. Chief Joseph returned word that he would talk. When General Miles came, Chief Joseph said, "From where the sun now stands I will fight no more, forever."

The two thousand mile ridicule of the U. S. military ended as he surrendered his gun to General Miles with a promise of fair treatment. Again, the United States Government broke its promise when they sent the tribe to Oklahoma rather than home to Idaho. The Army shot all of Chief Joseph's horses, believing without these animals, the Indians could now be controlled.

Traveling through Montana is beauty as if painted by an artist.

THE INDIAN DEMOCRACY

Indians form loose government hierarchies of chiefs, war chiefs, brave warriors, and family tribes or groups. Before anything was done the Indians would meet, talk, and decide as a group what action to take. They might unite or remain separate.

Chief Joseph's retreat was a masterpiece of genius, but his war chiefs were responsible for the victories over the military. They fought the military numerous times and mocked General Howard, Gibbon, Sturgis, and others during their travel of nearly two thousand miles.

The American press made Chief Joseph an American hero. It seemed the entire United States army and cavalry was sent west to conquer this small band of Indians marching to Canada rather than suffer the reservation. This attempt was one of the most highly regarded military accomplishments in the history of American Indian conflicts.

Chief Joseph was born in eastern Oregon in 1840, died in 1904, and was considered one of the Native American's great chiefs. Known as one of the greatest speakers of his time, his oratories were noble and often quoted. He said,

- *"The finest fur may cover toughest meat."*
- *"Cursed be the man that scalps the reputation of the dead."*
- *"The eye tells what the tongue would hide."*

He also said, *"The first white men of your people who came to our country were named Lewis and Clark. They brought many things our people had never seen. They talked straight, and our people gave them a great feast, as proof that their hearts were friendly. These men were kind, they made presents to our chiefs and our people made presents to them. We had many horses and gave them what they needed and they gave us guns and tobacco in return. All Nez Perce made friends with Lewis and Clark and agreed to let them pass through this country and never make war on white men. This promise the Nez Perce has never broken. Later your white men came to take the land, a little, then all. We only ask of your government to treat all men the same, as we came from the same mother."*

The story of the American Indian cannot be told any better than by the words of Chief Joseph.

CHAPTER 5
The Transition from Gold to Cowboys

The disappearing buffalo herds gave advent to a new industry, cattle ranching. Longhorns were the first of many breeds to be part of this new business.

THE MUSSELSHELL COUNTRY

The Musselshell River is a tributary of the Missouri River in central Montana. The river drains an area starting from the north side of the Crazy Mountains including the Castle Mountains and the south slopes of the Little Belts. As the drainage collects water, the river flows almost eastward, collecting the waters off the south side of the Big Snowy Mountains and the Little Snowy Mountains on its way to the Missouri. The river valley has eroded into gentle, rolling hills sloping down to river bottoms. Some of the best grass country in Montana is here.

The Indians came to the Musselshell for buffalo hunts and often to winter along the brown sandstone rimrocks. During the 1860s and 1870s cattlemen looked to the Musselshell with an eye for prosperity. The upper Musselshell was soon controlled by "Two Dot" Wilson. The Two Dot Ranch was operated from the Crazy Mountains to the mouth of the Musselshell River, a length and breadth of 260 miles by 60 miles. When "Two Dot" Wilson was asked how many cattle were under his brand, he did not know. He said, "I run good horses, lots of critters, and cowboys enough to bring 'em to market in the fall'."

John Murphy rode out on Locomotive Butte near the head of the Big Coulee and decided this is where he would locate his ranch. The ranch headquarters were just a few miles from Locomotive Butte, the year was 1879. The ranch was given the name "The 79 Ranch." In the foreground is the old Black homestead. These people filed on this homestead in 1912 and with barbed wire fences, the homesteaders ended free range in Montana.

JOHN T. MURPHY - CATTLE BARON

John Murphy started west from Missouri as a young man of twenty-one, freighting goods to the Virginia City gold diggers. Later, he rode out on a ridge called Locomotive Butte, and eyeing the land, stated "This is where I want my ranch." What he admired was a big coulee framed in saw-toothed rimrocks laying south of Ryegate, Montana and part of the Musselshell drainage. The year was 1879 and thereafter the ranch became the 79 Ranch. Parlaying his earnings wisely, he became owner of the Great Montana Cattle Company and while operating the 79 Ranch, built one of the most successful enterprises of his time. The "79" operation ran 40,000 cows and 70,000 sheep from the Big Coulee to the mouth of the Musselshell River. This ranch profited from 1879 to 1912 making millions of dollars utilizing free range. The 79 Ranch shipped six trainloads of steers in one season ... all going to the Chicago market.

The headquarters of the Two Dot Wilson Ranch on the Upper Musselshell River is now the town Two Dot, Montana, named after the cattle brand. This part of Montana along the Musselshell River is some of the most attractive ranch country in the West.

However, the colorful era of the cowboys and free range soon gave way to barbed wire and sodbusters around 1912. Murphy saw the end coming and started buying land, mostly from the railroad. Soon he controlled over 100 sections of prime Montana cow country in the Musselshell drainage. Today, the Big Coulee ranchers strip farm wheat and barley; cattle are grazed throughout the area.

Barbed wire fences closed off the free ranges of the west.

Charlie Bair came to Montana as a conductor on the Northern Pacific Railroad, liked what he saw and stayed the rest of his life. During his tenure in Montana, he was the largest sheep rancher in the world owning 300,000 head at one point in time.

East of Roundup, Montana, were other large cattlemen, H. Hightower, the N-Bar Ranch and others running thousands of head of cattle on the Big Dry, Little Dry, and the Lower Musselshell. One of the truly old ranches still operating is the N-Bar, headquartered on Flat Willow Creek coming out of the Little Snowy Mountains.

CHARLIE BAIR

The time of 1860 to 1912 was the west as portrayed in many western movies. During the end of this period, a man named Charlie Bair, famous around Billings, Montana, bought a ranch between the south and north forks of the Musselshell.

Charlie came west as a railroad conductor and used very good business sense to parlay the opportunities available in the west into one of the Montana great fortunes. The Bair Ranch today is in trust and harbors a museum for visitors to view the legacy left by one man coming west to make his fortune. Charlie was similar to Charlie Russell, the painter in that he was everyone's friend and was known from Portland, Oregon to Washington, D.C.

Charlie Bair was recognized as the largest sheep owner in the world running over 300,000 sheep during his time on the Crow Indian Reservation. Charlie once shipped an entire trainload of wool to Boston and at 24-5/8 cents per pound, totaled over $500,000.

Mr. Bair, always looking for what he called "the deal", sold his sheep when he heard about the Klondike Gold Strike. He took $100,000 to Seattle and helped perfect a perma-frost thawing machine to take to Alaska. Between his own claims and selling this machine, he brought a million dollars home for two years' work. This new money helped Charlie Bair dabble in many enterprises as he became one of Montana's most influential men. As his wealth grew, so did his fame.

Charlie, his wife and two daughters, were certainly part of the aristocracy of early Montana. The girls traveled to Europe, buying antique furniture and paintings for the Martinsdale ranch home. Alberta, the younger daughter, drove a large white convertible and with Charlie, raced horses and cars from Los Angeles to Seattle.

In the early years, major conflicts between the cattlemen and sheep herders started many range wars.

The Martinsdale Ranch, still in operation today, is typical of the early Montana ranches. These stockmen owned land as far as the eye could see. The lifestyle of these early men was open, friendly, and their homes were welcome to any traveler. They left a rich legacy to the State of Montana.

In 1907, the Musselshell Valley was invaded by the Milwaukee Railroad and with the railroad came homesteaders, irrigation, and the loss of free range. Some ranchers like John T. Murphy bought land from the railroad and with this ownership, stayed in business as a large operator for a while. Even the "79 Ranch," which had owned 100 sections, gradually was broken into smaller units.

The railroads needed goods to haul and the family farm seemed the answer. Small towns were built along the tracks every 20 to 40 miles and the railroad companies sponsored homesteading from St. Louis to the Pacific.

They moved goods freely from one coast to another making the west truly part of the United States. The wealth and the gross national income of America grew by compounding numbers and men like Charlie Bair, "Two Dot" Wilson, John T. Murphy, and Granville Stuart were forced to downsize.

The early history of the Musselshell Valley was buffalo and Indians, then cattle and sheep, followed by railroads and homesteaders, and now is a combination of all of these. The ghosts of the past are still showing in Castletown where a silver boom lasted only a few years. The abandoned road bed of the Milwaukee Railroad and the barbed wire fences depict the change from free range to family ranches.

Grain elevators were built every few miles along the railroad but today they are more central and handle unit trains of 54 cars.

The natural beauty of the Musselshell River Valley is serene and peaceful with a variety of river bottom pastures, grain elevators, low rolling grassy hills, and distant mountains framing many scenes. Every Montana art gallery showcases the past with oil paintings and bronze sculptures of Indians, cowboys, and the western life. The question is ... how do we now handle the future? American people are on the move again, leaving the city suburbs, moving back to rural Montana and the Musselshell Valley.

THE COWBOY

The Missouri River Country with its broad, flat prairies and grass stretching as far as the eye could see, was truly a stockman's dream. From 1882 to 1883 over 650,000 Longhorn cattle were trailed from the Pecos country of Texas to Montana, many ending up in the upper Missouri River country. It was not long before the Longhorn herds were resident cattle of Montana and cowboys worked year around for outfits such as the 79 Ranch, Two Dot, and others.

These cattle companies were always looking for men, and if a cowboy owned a slicker, bedroll, saddle, about six horses, and had the ability to rope and work cows, he was hired. It was a free life with more reality than romance. A man needed to be tough and tireless, with the nerves of the stone dead. He threw his saddle on the ground for a pillow and was up at daylight topping off a bronc. A cowboy could read the weather and the countryside like the back of his hand. The foreman never had to tell the man what work needed to be done. Western movies, books, and artists helped portray the life as more romantic than real.

Montana's free range ended with the onslaught of homesteaders and barbed wire. Many of the cowboys took residence in some part of the country they particularly liked and started ranches of their own near a spring or creek in a sheltered area. Even though free range was gone, the cowboy just changed to a cowman as he "took in" this rough country. The Missouri River country had miles of sod flats for homesteaders and many acres of rough, broken country for stockmen.

One of the early homesteaders turned horseman who made a living in this foreboding section of the west was Arnold Smith, now 93 years old. Like many Missourians from the

The West, as often thought, has been a reproduction made in Hollywood. The cowboy, cattle, and trail riding was only a short period in American history, but the movies, artists, and writers have extended its time. The reality of being an old-time cowboy was tough, lonesome, and without much glory.

Many a cowboy rode over the hill into a coulee and there before him was horse flesh he wished were in his string. Taking these animals meant swinging from a cottonwood tree, but, if he could change the brand...and move by night to another territory, he could gain top dollar.

midwest, Arnold's family migrated to Montana to homestead. They were latecomers and the only available land was in the Missouri Breaks. They settled on Wood Hawk Bench which possibly got its name from the steamboat era. The name wood hawk came from those men who cut, hauled, and stacked

Hidden away in the head of a canyon in the Missouri Breaks, this old corral has seen many horses and cows brands changed. From there, the stock went to Canada by night.

Arnold Smith, 93 years old, tells the story of old Montana during the time of outlaws, Longhorns, and running wild horses.

wood near the river to be sold as fuel for the paddlewheelers round tripping from St. Louis to Fort Benton.

Arriving in 1915, the Smith family filed on 320 acres of the Bench on the south side of the Missouri River thirty miles northeast of Winifred, Montana. Times were tough. Arnold said, "We were poor as church mice. We planted a garden and lived on the vegetables and the catfish we caught in the river. The game herds were nearly gone, killed off by market hunters, and the only cash crop we had was coyotes and bobcats trapped for $10 a pelt. In 1916 we traded for a milk cow giving the family milk, cream, and butter. We were the aristocrats of the Breaks."

Arnold learned at an early age to work hard and as a boy of eleven, hired out whenever he could find a job. It seemed only natural that Arnold and his brother, Ervin, began running, trading, and breaking wild horses. The Breaks were full of them by now because the Indian horses from the Belknap Indian Reservation on the north side of the river ran free. Arnold believes there were between 1,500 and 2,000 unbranded horses in the Breaks and as wild as deer, coyotes, or wolves.

It took a real horseman with a great horse to bunch these animals into a corral. Here, Arnold said, was where they were sorted and branded. The good were selected to be broke to the saddle, the outlaws were shipped as rodeo stock, and the rest were shipped to Chicago. Arnold made a small fortune over the years, working the horses and shipping as many as six carloads at one time to midwestern buyers. Later, he began raising registered Paint saddle stock, sought by horse owners throughout the west.

Arnold cares for thirty brood mares and they keep him young. At 93, when Arnold is asked about his success, he replies, "A horse trader buys right and sells to what someone will pay. I never sell a bad deal, but sure try my best to get the last penny." When asked what he would say if he could write his epitaph, he declared, "Arnold could do business anywhere on a handshake."

When asked if he rubbed elbows with any outlaws or tough guys, he said "Yes, several," and laughed. "Old George Middleton would steal anything, especially horses." Then Arnold launched into the story of Granville Stuart. "When the rustling was so bad in the Breaks, Stuart, Davis, and the Houser cow outfits decided to organize a vigilante group. They were called Stuart's stranglers."

When Wyoming, Colorado, and other states cleaned out the outlaw dens, the outlaws migrated to Montana. Arnold said the Breaks were full of them. The outlaw rustlers and horse thieves were blatant, operating from Lewistown, Montana to Canada. They rustled cattle in Montana, drove them to Canada and sold them, then stole Canadian horses to trail back to the United States. Edward "Long Hair" Owens and Charles "Rattlesnake" Fallon were as rotten as any pirates on the Caribbean Sea.

The vigilantes, led by a gunman named Barnett, were a match. Arnold tells, "They rode through the Breaks shooting and hanging anyone who appeared to be a rustling outlaw." He laughed and continued, "The rope didn't know the difference between good and bad. If

Arnold Smith, as a boy, lived near the Missouri River on Woodhawk Bench. This area of Montana was lonesome country. Some say they would step out of the cabin just to listen to the wind blow. Not many travelers ventured into this broken canyon country.

you were in bad company ... it was too late." Within a few weeks the hanging claimed men like Narciss Lavardure, Bill McKenzie, Billy Downs, "California" Ed, and about twenty-three in all. The townspeople in Lewistown killed "Long Hair" Owens and "Rattlesnake" Fallon. Rattlesnake was hit with nine bullets

The Vigilantes rode through the Breaks looking for rustlers to hang. If you were in the wrong company, your neck was stretched along with the bad.

In the short time the Vigilantes were riding the Breaks, they hung 23 men and the outlaws who survived, soon disappeared.

and Owens, eleven. They were the ringleaders of an outlaw gang operating from Rocky Point north of the Missouri River.

The remaining outlaws were soon headed for greener pastures and the Missouri Breaks were again left for the honest folks raising families. Cow outfits like Stuart, Davis, and Houser ran about 40,000 head of cattle in the Breaks. Others like "Two Dot" Wilson, H. Hightower, and Murphy of the "79" Ranch, could now bring in a calf crop. This lasted until 1911 when the horde of sodbusters came.

Arnold tells the story about his old friend, Jack Ervin, who was run out of Texas by a posse and ended up hiding in the Breaks. Jack told Arnold, "We were pinned down in the big thicket with the posse firing. We hugged the ground tight 'til dark, then lit out not to come back." Afterwards Jack laid stake to some grassland south of the Bearpaw Mountains and left to get some cattle from the lower country. When he came back trailing his herd, he found Nels Nelson, a sheepherder, had moved in and mowed the grass clean to the ground. Jack put out the word the country was not big enough for him and Nelson, and he had better move on. A few days later, the foolish herder showed up with his bunch of sheep and a 30-30 rifle in the crook of his arm. Jack shot him and left him to rot in the dirt. The country had Jack up for murder and the trial date was set. Cattlemen showed up from all over for the trial and it took the judge only minutes to acquit —- not enough evidence for murder. Arnold said, "Jack was an honest man, but stay on his good side," and then he chuckled.

When men like Arnold pass, another era of Montana history will be gone.

Transportation in the Missouri River Country

The Missouri River country was miles from St. Louis, Salt Lake City, San Francisco, and Portland. Travel was long and tiring. First, the fur trappers came by canoe and keel boats up the Missouri and Yellowstone rivers, later, by paddle wheelers, mule trains, stage coaches, and finally by railroad. The steel rails made the Missouri Country accessible to everyone.

by Rene' - Courtesy Burl Jones Art Gallery, Livingston, Montana

CHAPTER 6
Transportation into the Missouri River Country

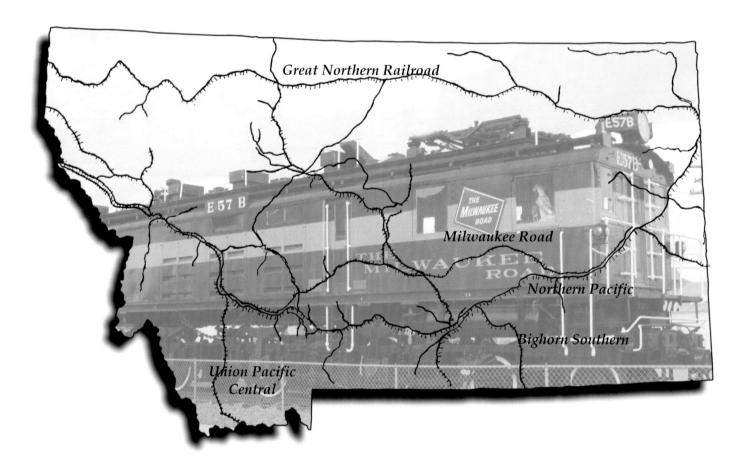

Great Northern Railroad

Milwaukee Road

Northern Pacific

Bighorn Southern

Union Pacific Central

Starting in 1880, the railroads crisscrossed Montana to capture the lucrative hauling of natural resources to the eastern markets.

The old freight wagons, pulled by horses or mules, were very limited in the cargo that they could haul. Salt Lake City was the nearest origination of goods for the gold mines of southern Montana.

The 1860's brought gold mining, and the beginning of the cattle industry. The '70's saw silver, lead, copper, and the demand for better transportation. The '80's, '90's and turn of the century railroads dissected North Dakota and Montana with spurs to the major economic points.

The character of the prairie is symbolized by the Yucca blooming in June. This flower may be the tallest plant to be seen for miles and miles.

RIVERBOATS

At the age of twelve, Grant Marsh signed on as a cabin boy on the Dover, a riverboat which ran the Ohio River. Afterward, came a succession of jobs until he became a riverboat pilot and captain. His dream of running the Missouri River began as a deck hand on a trip from St. Louis to St. Joseph on the Missouri. The muddy Missouri was considered the toughest American river for a paddlewheel captain to navigate. Snags, floating logs, sand bars and muddy waters made the treacherous channels difficult to read and tough to keep out of trouble. Flooding conditions could change the river channel overnight, causing the gravel bars to shift one direction or another. Marsh mentally practiced the route through the hazards along the 2,000 mile trip from St. Louis to Fort Benton. Captain Grant Marsh was soon recognized as a great pilot, extremely capable of guiding his paddlewheeler through the troubled, muddy waters of the Missouri.

The 1862 gold strikes in the Montana Territory at Grasshopper Creek, Virginia City, Last Chance Gulch, and others placed a premium on the Missouri riverboat traffic. The number of boats increased many times - 70 steam paddlewheelers annually arrived at Fort Benton carrying 20,397,000 pounds of cargo. This coincided with Captain Marsh's prime as a boat captain. He spent late spring, summer, and early fall carrying miners, tools, clothes, and food up river to Fort Benton on his paddlewheeler, the *Luella*. Down river, the *Luella* carried gold, passengers, hides, and furs. During one trip, the boat hauled over one million

courtesy of Hall Diteman

The wild and muddy Missouri River was a nightmare for navigation and many shallow bottom river boats hit snags and sandbars.

dollars in gold to St. Louis, considered the third U.S. port. The port handled 3,000 riverboats annually during the high-use period.

During the 1860's and 1870's, the Indians felt the intense pressure of the white-miner hordes and the Indian wars began. The boat cargos changed to military...guns, supplies, food, and soldiers were dropped upstream at forts along the Missouri and Yellowstone rivers. Captain Marsh became the man of choice for military generals Terry, Custer, Miles, and Keogh to run the rivers. When he received orders to travel up the Yellowstone River, Captain Marsh replaced his large paddlewheeler with a

smaller riverboat, the *Far West*. This boat, with a shallow draft and extra power, allowed Captain Marsh to cruise the Yellowstone. One trip he carried General Custer and General Terry up the Yellowstone River to Miles City, Montana and then continued up the Bighorn River to the mouth of the Little Bighorn River. Here he was to wait until after the confrontation with the Sioux during the Battle of the Little Bighorn.

General Custer and General Terry received orders in early 1876 to march, subdue the Sioux Indians, and force them to return to reservations. Captain Marsh provided the vital military support of supplies, food, and other necessities which he dropped at points along the Yellowstone River.

Indian warriors, waiting in the grass, jumped and killed all two hundred and eight soldiers including General Custer in the Battle of the Little Bighorn. Other units were attacked also, but were not all killed. After several days of siege, the Indians left. After the famous battle, the wounded were to be transported by the *Far West*. They were taken to the mouth of the Little Bighorn. Captain Marsh made the fastest known trip down the Bighorn River to the Yellowstone and Missouri rivers to Fort Abraham to deliver the wounded to the army hospital.

Captain Marsh lived up to his name "King of the Muddy Missouri." The *Far West* made the trip in 54 hours, averaging 15 miles per hour traveling 810 miles of shallow, treacherous rivers.

The Battle of the Little Bighorn occurred in July, 1876. Within seven short years, the railroad arrived at Billings, Montana during the summer of 1883. This heralded the finale of the riverboats on the Yellowstone and soon silenced the boats on the Upper Missouri.

THE COMING OF THE RAILROAD

The Bozeman Trail shot off the Oregon Trail, crossed north of the Bighorn Mountains along the Yellowstone River to Bozeman, Montana. The Sioux, led by Red Cloud, shut down this route shortly after its opening. Treaty after treaty was violated by the U. S. Government concerning travel through the buffalo hunting country of northeastern Wyoming. The Bozeman Trail would be a shorter route to the new Montana gold fields.

The distant new country of the upper Missouri River lay miles from St. Louis and San Francisco and travel into the area was long and arduous. The paddlewheelers established ports along the Missouri from 1832 to 1883. Overland stagecoaches and freight lines came

The first railroad line into Montana was a spur off the Union Pacific Central to Butte, Montana, and then the above Butte Anaconda Western was a spur to Virginia City. Passenger trains hit the end of the line when the gold played out.

The western canyons and mountain passes were expensive construction for the railroad companies. Many companies went broke and were reorganized several times before they finally became economically viable.

from Salt Lake City to Bannack and Virginia City around 1862 after the gold strike. No matter the route travelers chose or how they traveled into the upper Missouri River country from 1805 to 1883. Travel was difficult and time consuming. With the advent of the railroad in 1883 the Missouri River country bloomed overnight.

The first railroad was a spur off the Union Pacific Central from Salt Lake City into the Dillon-Butte, Montana area. This line primarily hauled ores from the Butte-Anaconda mining operations to the east. Simultaneously, Henry Villard was building the Northern Pacific from Portland eastward and Frederick Billings was building the Northern Pacific westward, arriving at Bozeman, Montana in 1883. This part of the west, with connecting railroad lines to both coasts, created a flourishing economy, and with two railroads, prices dropped making the economics more favorable.

The Union Pacific was given land grants and money by the U. S. Government. The Northern Pacific received only large land grants, 40 sections of land per mile of track in Montana and 20 sections in Minnesota and Oregon. Railroads were capital consuming and up-front the money was needed. Building trestles, tracks, grades, purchasing equipment and payroll called for cash on the barrel head. Large bond sales were held to raise money, but the slightest waiver in the national economy created panic with the purchasers. A number of railroad bankruptcies resulted from overspending in an effort to be the first to complete a route. The railroads created business ventures to attract new people, but before the profits could help, the backers would stall, creating panic. This meant the railroads sold their land grants to raise money any way possible, but often it wasn't fast enough to keep these big companies solvent. Therefore, the railroads were often headed for reorganization and within a time frame of ten years, a railroad company might have changed ownership several times. The mineral riches of the new west (gold, silver, zinc, lead, and copper) could easily be shipped to the eastern industries once the railroad companies stabilized. The 1890s became the heyday for

Modern shippers from foreign countries place their cargo in containers. When the units arrive in the United States, they are downloaded onto flat cars. The railroads then head for various locations across the United States.

the railroads, and they provided the United States and the Missouri River country an era of golden growth.

The Northern Pacific Railroad through Montana whetted the appetite of investors. The next big venture was the Great Northern headed by James Hill. The road crossed the high line of northern Montana and opened up the Milk River Valley, as well as square miles of prairie land for dry land farming. New towns sprung up along the tracks - Culbertson, Glasgow, Malta, Scobey, and others stretching across 500 miles of this vacant country. And, from the Great Northern, spurs were laid south into Great Falls, Helena, and Butte. The Great Northern was new competition forcing freight rates to drop, creating an even more favorable economic climate.

Dynamos of their time, Villard, Hill, and Billings were taking great risks with the hope of big rewards and spurred the building of these large transportation companies. The railroad reigned king for a number of years until World War II when the government began building freeways. This provided roads for semi-trucks to convey goods with greater ease and convenience. Ocean-going ships were loaded with containers to be unloaded on to trains, later to be transferred to trucks in Chicago or St. Louis. Today, goods move effortlessly everywhere, and the United States has become the most mobile country in the world.

Big changes came quickly after World War II for the poorly organized railroads, but now with new adjustments the companies are viable businesses once again.

Since World War II, trucking on American freeways brings goods to every city in America. This convenience of delivery has made the trucking industry a business rivaling the railroads.

Our modern freeways move traffic from coast-to-coast with ease.

History considers Chief Plenty Coups a visionary. The Chief's handling of the American White government was skillful and he negotiated the largest acreage of reservation in the northern states.

BIG BUSINESS WHEELING AND DEALING

Many big deals were made behind closed doors concerning just how and where the railroads would extend their influence.

One of these so called big deals was punching the Burlington Railroad from the midwest through Wyoming to cross the Crow Indian Reservation and join with the Northern Pacific Railway at Huntley, Montana.

This would give the Burlington Railroad access to the Pacific without the cost of building a line from the Yellowstone River to the ocean. This portion of the railroad coming through Sheridan, Wyoming was called the Bighorn Southern. The time was early 1880's with many companies trying to capture the lucrative trade of hauling materials from the

eastern factories to the West and hauling raw materials on the return trip.

During railroad expansion, these moguls of big business were accused of collusion, monopoly, and price fixing. The Northern Pacific Railroad avoided these criticisms by allowing the Bighorn Southern to join and use its rails.

During the late 1870's and early 1880's, the Crow Indian Reservation was established and this two-million acre area was directly in the path of the proposed Bighorn Southern Line.

The Crow Indians were generally peaceful with the United States and were awarded the largest of reservations in Montana. The railroad needed to obtain a signed document allowing right-of-way across Indian lands.

The right-of-way needed by the Bighorn Southern was 101.75 miles from the ghost town of Aberdeen, Montana near the Wyoming border, to join the Northern Pacific at the Yellowstone River, now Huntley, Montana.

Once the planned route was approved by Congress, the railroad needed to obtain an agreement with the Indians. Deals do not happen fast with the Indians, and this parley took a year, finally being signed April 25, 1894.

The Mid-continent Railroad (Grand Island, Northern Wyoming, and the Bighorn Southern) when in connection with the Northern Pacific would complete a large integrated transportation system serving central United States. This cooperative rail line would give economic power to both companies.

THE CROW INDIAN PARLEY

The Indian Council, comprised of 135 Crow Indians, was not easily convinced that the railroad should be allowed. First the railroad offered $1.25 for each acre. The Indians did not comprehend what an acre of land encompassed or how wide the right-of-way would be. Finally it was agreed that 25 steps each way would be the right-of-way.

Then Chief Spotted Horse asked $2.00 an acre. Finally, Chief Plenty Coups asked for

$3.00 per acre and it was agreed.

Spotted Horse negotiated 50 cents for each tree cut for ties on the reservation and the railroad right-of-way fenced to avoid killing cows and horses.

Next, before any sod was cut, the tribe insisted they be paid for the right-of-way. They also wished to ride the train free of fare, and finally the railroad was to haul coal for use in Indian homes. The signing took place under the watchful eye of Paul McCormick, with the approval of J.J. Morgan, Commissioner of Indian Affairs.

Mining, Cattle & Homesteads

The cow became king and wheat the staff of life.

The railroads expanded the West by taking raw materials to market. The new markets created expanding businesses...mining, cattle, sheep, and farming. Families came from all parts of the world to find work and make a home in the Missouri Country.

CHAPTER 7
Mining, Cattle and Homesteading in the Missouri River Country

Early miners left their junk strewn across the countryside.

Dredge mining for gold left the streambeds ruined for hundreds of years.

The world has been very critical of early mining, especially in Montana. These men, in reality, came, took, and left the countryside scarred for years. Their abandoned old machinery marred the beauty of the northern Rockies.

The Asarco plant of East Helena has been in operation since 1899. Here lead ores and concentrates from Canada, South America, Australia, Asia, and many states in the U.S. are remanufactured for final sale.

MINING

During the 1860's, 70's and 80's, there existed no regulations. The pristine environments were turned topsy-turvy, water was polluted, and no effort was made to replace soils. The miners came like locusts, and had the effect of a large tornado, striking and twisting as they carved the hillsides, dredged stream beds, and then were suddenly gone in the night.

Today the story sings a better song; grass and trees are replanted and topsoils are replaced. Tailing materials are hauled back into the mine shafts and the openings are resealed. Chemical pollutants are collected in sealed ponds, water is recycled, and chemicals extracted and reused. Miners have developed more improved methods to care for our environment.

Copper Ore

North Dakota and eastern Montana have immense coal beds. These layers were laid down millions of years ago during the Mesozoic era. Large flats were covered by shallow seas and swamps and the materials deposited over eons of time collected to become carbon fuel beds. Today, both North Dakota and Montana have large strip mining operations and move millions of tons of coal annually. Some coal is used for on-site electrical power plants, and some shipped by rail to eastern utility markets. The coal-powered plants produce great quantities of electricity which is pushed into the national grid traveling through high voltage lines to illuminate towns and cities.

Tilted strata of rock created by the mountain orogeny.

The same shallow seas and swamps harbored billions of small diatoms, algae and other one cell creatures. As they died the carbon residue of their bodies collected as liquids and migrated to hidden pockets in the earth. Petroleum geologists call these pools Lodgepole, Red River, and Mission Canyon, meaning where oil and gas is found in certain porous strata.

In the Missouri River Country, oil and gas is extracted from many areas ... Williston Basin, Cut Bank, Baker, naming but a few. Although coal, oil, and gas have similar characteristics, coal is formed from plants; oil and gas from animals. When the compression of the tectonic plates began to push the horizontal strata toward each other this action caused mountain stacking. Deep subterranean mineral deposits were tilted upwards exposing layer after layer of rare metals. These are termed ores and were available for extraction in the Rocky Mountain area. Very rare metals such as platinum and palladium are found and the Stillwater Mining Company extracts these compounds for U.S. markets. Only three places in the world produce these rare metals for use in catalytic converters for automobiles and conductors for computers, making this mine very important to the U.S. economy.

NEW METAL MINING

Gold first brought the miners, but soon silver, lead, zinc, copper, limestone, and bentonite became the economic power base. This bountiful supply of these mineral resources was carried by railroads to eastern industrial centers, and vaulted the U.S. into a world dominant power. Cities like Pittsburgh, Cleveland, and others became manufacturing complexes rivaling any found in Europe.

Today, mining represents jobs, taxes for cities, churches, and schools. Yesteryear, miners ran roughshod over the country, but now the industry has gained a new respect for the countryside and is more interwoven into the economy.

THE RANCH

The western ranch contained headquarters, corrals, bunkhouse, and home - a place where everyone wished their children to grow. Often the headquarters were situated in the bottoms near a stream where winter feed for the livestock was most abundant. Spring grass sprouted here first, then stair-stepped up the mountains as summer came on. Range preservation was part of ranching as well as management of the cow herd. If the grass was gone, calves sold "light" in the fall so pastures

Typically, a ranch may have livestock, dryland wheat and feed crops growing under irrigation, however some farmers began to specialize raising wheat and dry land barley. Larger powerful tractors were manufactured to pull all the equipment needed to complete the operation in one or two passes over the land. Dryland farms encompassed more acres as these big tractors came into use. The production of wheat grew in volumes exceeding all expectations. Market glut became the common rather than the unusual.

Montana heaven is seeing your range cow standing belly deep in wild yellow sweet clover.

were defined to rotate the cattle from low grounds and gradually climbing the mountain slopes as summer came. The lower areas then grew back for fall and winter pasture.

Often winding through the meadow was a beautiful trout stream where the fish population was always protected by taking only enough for supper. Hunting was customarily handled much the same way - shoot only what would be eaten.

After the great, free-range ranches of the 1880s vanished, the smaller family-size ranch emerged in the Missouri River country. Family homes were scattered across the miles of prairie along streams and other favorable places.

Families had to stick together like glue to survive two world wars, several severe depressions, and the unsteady agricultural economy. After World War II, the government began to control the surpluses of wheat with allotments and price subsidies, yet farmers still produced the cheapest food in the world for the American people. Federal control served the short term need but often proved very laborious. Grain crops of wheat, barley, and corn came under the most scrutiny.

The family farm seemed destined for dissolution as the problems mounted. Bigger and better equipment was manufactured, allowing small family farms to encompass

The old dirt road across the prairie was an eternity to travel, miles of nothing but fence posts and the billowing of distant clouds.

Time was unimportant, hurrying did not seem to have much care.

A cottontail would break the minute while a bounding coyote might take more, but when the prairie was green, the beauty would soak through and through.

For here the moment gave time to absorb the breeze, and the stretch of miles, as if nowhere was everywhere.

The Prairie

hundreds of acres. The lean years kept spending close to the belt, but the fierce sense of independence seems to be worth the effort. Whether the operation raises sheep, cows, wheat, or feed, the market remains out of the grower's control making success uncertain. The Missouri Country is in the marginal rainfall belt and drought is always present. The saying was "This country is five minutes away from mud and only two hours from dust."

After World War II, tractors sold for $3,500; today they sell for $135,000. A pickup worth $3,000 in 1949 now sells for $30,000. A bushel of wheat brought $5 to $6 in 1950; today $4.50 is a good price. A fat calf would bring $.80 a pound in the fall of 1955, but today it might bring only $.50 to $.60 a pound.

Cattle ranches fared better than sheep operations, because the cow looked too big for a coyote to eat. By 1920, most of the wolves were exterminated, and beef became the choice of meat in America, especially after World War II. Backyard grills for burgers or steaks became standard equipment on city-dweller patios. This added to the mystique of owning a western cattle ranch ... a fantasy carried out in numerous western movies. Montana's own Gary Cooper fit the mold perfectly in the movie *High Noon*.

The prairie rattler was everybody's enemy. But in reality, he was more afraid of humans than they were of him.

At a glance, the prairie appears lifeless. The prairies are miles of grassland stretched across the skyline from North Dakota to the Rocky Mountains, Here the rattlesnake, the prairie dog, antelope and a multitude of other animals and plants flourish. The profusion of small flowering plants add radiance to the dull green summer grasses stretching as far as the eye can see.

The true monarch of the prairie is the cottonwood tree. In June, when the tree blooms, thousands of white puffs with seeds are scattered in the wind creating a summer snow storm.

The prairie line is broken by these trees growing along stream bottoms stretching for miles wherever the water flows. The plant consumes gallons of water every day. A summertime picnic in a cottonwood grove, cool with a slight breeze is a Montana memory.

Windmills stand above the prairie symbolizing new life as 'water' was added to the semi-arid landscape. The paddles turned slowly in the breeze, or faster in the wind, but always lifting some amounts of fluid to provide for the family and livestock.

The Indians of North Dakota, especially the Mandan and Hidatsa, were agriculturalists raising beans, squash, pumpkins, and corn. Indian tribes from Montana, Canada, and Wyoming came to trade for these foods. Thus, North Dakota should be considered the cradle of Missouri River agriculture.

The first white farmers were fur traders and missionaries around forts. These crops were vegetables, some grain, and livestock. However, in the Bitterroot Valley, Jesuit priests at St. Mary's used irrigation to raise potatoes, vegetables, and wheat. They also built and operated a flour mill.

Since the Plains Indians of Montana, Wyoming, and Utah country were basically nomadic, agriculture did not begin until the mining camp's demand for food.

Dryland wheat yields are in direct relationship to rainfall.

AGRICULTURE

The Missouri River is farmed from the mountain valleys to St. Louis, and each tributary contributes. The broad plains spread from Canada to Colorado. Crops are irrigated along the river bottoms, dryland wheat and barley is grown on expansive prairies, and livestock is grazed in the rough, broken country.

The movement of glaciers down from the Arctic helped create these large flats stretching from the Rocky Mountains to the Red River in North Dakota and the large, glacial lakes helped spread eroded materials across miles and miles of land, especially north and east of Great Falls, Montana.

The dryland farmer has one eye on the sky and one hand on the Bible, praying for rain.

During bountiful crop years, the prices fall and farmers say if the right hand doesn't get you, the left hand will.

Promoters of the west sold dreams to the dryland farmers. At the height of the land boom, 1916, Montana's population was 769,590 - almost the same as it is today. The ebb and flow of Montana's population has been tied to the harvest of its resources: furs, mining, agriculture, timber, and land. However, the state remains sparsely populated with only 5.5 people per square mile, while North Dakota boasts 9.3 people per square mile.

In 1902, after much urging from Governor Joseph K. Toole, U.S. Senator Thomas H. Carter, and a promoter from Billings, the federal government passed the Newlands Reclamation Act. These irrigation projects turned large blocks of semi-desert areas into cropland able to grow sugar beets, corn, wheat barley, potatoes, and alfalfa. These products became the backbone of agriculture.

Rocky Mountain waters are used for irrigation, helping grow crops...seed potatoes, alfalfa hay, sugar beets, and sunflowers.

MILK RIVER DRAINAGE

The Milk River begins its flow off the icy crags of east Glacier National Park. This eastern face of the Rocky Mountains is as rough and desolate as any from Alaska to Central America. Geologists believe that prior to the Ice Age the Missouri flowed northward to empty into Hudson Bay. Ice dams changed the river's course and one of its old channels is where the Milk River flows today. The Milk River Valley is much wider than normal for a stream its size and the fertile bottom lands on each side is ideal agricultural land, especially if irrigation is applied. Flat prairies on both sides of the river stretch for miles north, south, and east. These grasslands were home to large herds of buffalo, then cattle and sheep, and now are dryland grain farms.

The first humans in this area were the Assiniboine, Gros Ventre, Blackfeet, Cree, Sioux, and the Crow Indians. These people lived a nomadic life following buffalo herds and gathering plant foods. Before acquiring horses, dogs were used to pull the travois, helping to move the tepees from place to place. The grass was rich and the large game populations offered a good life for these Indians. After acquiring the horse during the early 1700s, tribes could find food easier and live an even more nomadic lifestyle.

Meriwether Lewis and a few of his men explored the Marias River on their return trip from Oregon to St. Louis. The party camped with a small band of Blackfeet warriors, who during the night attempted to steal guns, horses and supplies. Two braves were killed by the Americans during the skirmish. This encounter caused deep resentment with the Blackfeet Indians and from 1805 to about 1850, the Blackfeet declared the Americans an enemy. The French-Canadians and British ventured west in Blackfeet country earlier, but this was the first American contact. The Indians continued their trade with the British,

The broad Milk River Valley is the old Missouri River Valley. Glaciers pushed the Missouri flow 50 to 70 miles to the south. The Milk River looks diminutive flowing through this broad valley.

but not the Americans. Even then, all whites were guests only in their lands.

After the 1855 treaty between the Americans and the Blackfeet Indians, whites began to move into the rich grasslands north of the Missouri River. First they hunted buffalo for hides and tongues. The hides were shipped by riverboat and the tongues were pickled for the eastern markets. Next came the migratory cattle and sheep herds, and during this era the riverboats began to bring miners and supplies to Fort Benton.

The Great Northern Railroad arrived in the Milk River Valley in 1887 and with the railroad came the homesteaders. The first homestead act issued 160 acres, but in this area, most people did not believe a farm this size could support a family. In 1907, the U. S. Government changed the issue to 320 acres

The broad, flat prairies of the Milk River country stretch for miles and miles. The early homesteads started at 320 acres but gradually, as crop failures, insects, and low prices weeded out the weak, these farms became as large as the country.

and settlers began to arrive and file. Towns like Glasgow, Malta, Chinook, Chester, and Cut Bank sprang up like weeds along the railroad. With the towns came churches, schools, and mercantile stores. The Indians were forced onto reservations as 156,988 homestead filings were made between 1909 and 1920 bringing the white population to 220,000 people.

The dryland homestead farms were subject to drought, freeze, insects, and hailstorms. Some farmers made it, many did not. Gradually, the farms became bigger as new machinery, fertilizers, and better methods helped those remaining to become successful business people.

The first railroads used wood for steam energy, then later coal became the fuel of choice. Here in the Milk River country were vast coal beds laid down millions of years ago when inland seas and swamps covered from the Arctic to the Gulf of Mexico. Coal was mined and sold for $3.50 a ton delivered for homes, businesses, factories, and the railroad.

Next came the discovery of oil in the 1920's and fuel oils began to replace coal. Crude oil was refined for sale as gasoline, which was used in the newfangled autos and trucks. This brought the modern era into full swing. The valley, with electricity, gasoline, diesel, irrigation, and prairies of dryland farms furnished American markets with wheat, barley, sugar beets, cattle, and sheep. The Milk River Valley is diverse in agricultural products.

The subterranean treasure of oil and gas was found in the 1920's. This new fuel source helped boost the economy of the entire region.

Irrigated corn is grown for livestock feed in the Missouri River drainage.

Travel, Recreation, and Sightseeing

courtesy of the Hole in the Wall Gallery Ennis, Montana

The upper Missouri River tributaries...the Gallatin and the Madison rivers...begin in Yellowstone Park. The Madison River, after collecting several small streams, flows northwest to help form the Missouri River.

By collecting mineral riches from Yellowstone Park Hot Springs, the waters are some of the world's best trout streams. Big Rainbows, Browns, and Cutthroats give fly fishermen recreation of a lifetime.

CHAPTER 8
Travel, Recreation, and Sightseeing

Rocky Mountain limestone strata with percolating waters often form vast caverns running long distances underground. The Lewis and Clark Caverns are a "must visit" while traveling through Montana.

Plan your visits to

- *Lewis & Clark Caverns*

- *Yellowstone Falls*

- *Glacier National Park*

Early lava flows of the Yellowstone volcanoes left the colorful graphic creations, Yellowstone Falls and Yellowstone Canyon.

Yellowstone National Park, the North American hot spot, has many underground chambers where water is super-heated in old volcanic vents creating some 10,000 hot springs and geysers. One of the largest geyser areas is at the headwaters of the Madison river.

THE MISSOURI FLYWAY FOR WATERFOWL

Geologists think life on earth began in the Protozoic Era about 2.5 billion years ago.

Many fossils have been found in Missouri River areas, as the uplifting of the mountains exposed much of the earth's early history.

The rising of the Rocky Mountains began interfering with rainfall, and the east side of the mountains became semi-arid desert. This helped preserve fossils of these early periods.

Many museums here in the Missouri drainage have fossil displays and field trips can be arranged.

These studies show how many species flourished, then became extinct, as food chains and weather had affected their being. Changing environments were happening throughout geologic history.

Today, we have some acceleration of environmental changes which need to be slowed down or reversed.

• Water pollution by pesticides and other contaminants must be reversed.

• Drainage of wetlands has a major effect on migratory birds...ducks, geese, snipes, and these areas need protection.

• Care must be taken to maintain natural pollenators of plants... honey bees, wild bees, and birds, etc.

Today, with large equipment, ecosystems can be altered. Our lives on earth are interwoven with other creatures sharing the planet. Protecting their environment is important, while still maintaining a viable economy.

Wetlands are home to thousands of species of birds, insects, and plants. Their health is an indication of the water purity.

When sightseeing in the Missouri River Country, watch for the upland birds.

The Chinese Ring-necked Pheasant moved right in with humans and made himself at home.

Meadowlarks are a prairie bird and each morning sing a happy song.

ROCKY MOUNTAIN BIGHORN SHEEP

The Rocky Mountain bighorn sheep are the most coveted trophy of western America. The animal grows large horns which reach full curl with maximum thickness about his eighth year. This magnificent creature of the high wind-swept grass slopes of the Rocky Mountains survives in Mother Nature's harshest conditions. He can hop from rock to rock, defying gravity and mastering treacherous footing. This beautiful specie of North American animals is tough, yet delicate.

When Lewis and Clark came, the bighorn sheep was found in habitat from Culbertson, Montana along the Missouri Breaks throughout the Rocky Mountains proper.

They were seen everywhere as the expedition recorded finding these beautiful animals in great herds occupying the most treacherous of areas. During the first fifty years, the herds were holding their own, but when domesticated sheep and the market hunters came, the herds began to dwindle. During the early part of the 1900's, their numbers declined to near extinction with some subgroups disappearing altogether. The "Audubon bighorn" disappeared in 1916 when the last animal was shot. For thousands of years, these animals adjusted to subzero winters, sparse vegetation and most curves that nature could throw. Lungworm from domestic sheep, overgrazing, and hunting reduced the numbers below the ability of the species to reproduce. Like many groups they have become nearly extinct.

Today, the fish and game commissions of North Dakota and Montana have replenished herds in the Missouri Breaks areas, especially in the Charles Russell Wildlife Refuge and in the Little Missouri Badlands. Some groups are doing well, but others are barely clinging to existence.

This story is typical of many species living here. The grizzly bear population has dwindled, threatened with extinction as inbreeding reduces the gene pools. The buffalo are now multiplying in certain areas, but for a time were reduced to a very few small isolated herds. These species evolved over thousands of years without major predators... until the arrival of man. Maintaining a healthy habitat for these animals will take dedication and ingenuity on all levels.

GLACIER NATIONAL PARK

St. Mary's Lake was formed by glacial action approximately 20,000 years ago. The reflections in the lake illustrate the picturesque beauty of east Glacier National Park.

Single Shot Mountain clearly illustrates where the gray Appekunny Formation slid over the top of the Altyn limestone strata.

GLACIER NATIONAL PARK

The natural splendor created by the formation of the Rocky Mountains makes East Glacier, without exception, one of the most unique places in North America. Logan Pass traversed by the "Going-to-the-Sun" Highway represents the drainage boundary of water flowing eastward off the northern Rockies. East Glacier's poetic scenery of lakes, streams, glaciers, and sheer rock mountain walls is a great and humbling experience.

The geologic time book has been opened up here by the thrusting and faulting, showing off millions of years of the earth's surface formation. During the Cretaceous Period of the Mesozoic Era, the compression of plates occurred and some upthrusts reached 10,448 feet high.

The many mountain peaks of Glacier Park are sedimentary formations pushed upward. This happened approximately 70 million years ago.

Many mountain tops are over 8,000 feet. This compression of the Pacific Plate into and under the Continental Plate exposed sedimentary and metamorphic rock dating back approximately one billion six hundred million years.

East Glacier is a fascinating classroom of geology and the beautiful splendor of each view captures everyone's interest. A family trip into Glacier National Park from the east is a delight. First one beholds St. Mary Lake, so clear that mountain reflections are like paintings... masterpieces each one. Starting with Single Shot Mountain, where the Appekunny Formation lays over the Altyn dolomites and limestone, then across the lake is Red Eagle Mountain and so many others.

The bright red Grinnell Formation illustrates how water formed these rocks millions of years ago.

The geological formations are close to the edge of the road, and clearly show how water formed these rocks millions of years ago. After viewing the limestone formations, a view of the Appekunny is just steps away. On the "Going-the-the-Sun" Highway, is the red Grinnell Formation named after the famous American writer George Bird Grinnell. Again, this formation shows how waters carried silts, clays, and other minerals to deposit layer after layer of sandstone to gradually become rock. Even the ripples in the old muds are preserved, reflecting time, perhaps 600 million years ago. These natural expressions are like an open book, accentuated with wild flowers, fall colors, and a variety of wild life...perhaps even a grizzly bear, so bring binoculars!

Six hundred million years ago running water formed the ripples, now rock, exposed along the "Going-to-the-Sun" Highway, Glacier National Park.

Blue Lupine is one of the many flowers coloring the natural landscape in Glacier National Park.

The Rocky Mountains abound in wild flowers. More than 5,000 species grow and bloom each year. These plants brighten any day.

Tired of traveling...
stop and see a rodeo!

Painted in liquid motion: the riding of a bronc used to be a Saturday afternoon event at the county picnic. Today, it is big business in indoor or outdoor arenas. The bucking stock are big, tough animals putting the modern cowpoke at the disadvantage. He's lucky to last 8 seconds and not eat ground or be stomped on by 1400 pounds of horse.

Family fun is everywhere and public lands are scattered throughout the Missouri River Country. Hiking, trail riding, fishing, and many sports are available all year long.

Missouri River Small Towns and Cities

Lewistown is nestled in central Montana, somewhat isolated, and from the town's beginning its illustrious history typifies Montana all over again. The Charlie Russell history is evident everywhere here as the Judith River gathers water from the Little Belts and the Big Snowy Mountains to flow northward to the Missouri. First it was just cattle scattered over the grassy hills, then came the gold miners into Maiden Basin of the Judith Mountains.

Wheat is now grown over square miles of what was once prairie land. This quiet sleepy town enjoys one of the better annual rainfalls of this semi-arid desert region. Rough lands still ranch cattle and the plateau flats are strip farmed as far as the eye can see. Large elevators store grain, while trucks take calves to feeders in Colorado, Nebraska, and Iowa.

CHAPTER 9
Missouri River Small Towns and Cities

DILLON, MONTANA

DILLON ... home of the Bulldogs and Western Montana College, is a small city where history is frozen in time. The beautiful Beaverhead River, where Lewis and Clark traversed in August 1805, is a fine trout stream, and cattle, hay, and livestock are produced in abundance in the valley. Dillon's atmosphere is quiet, like listening to a beautiful songbird beginning his morning warbling in a land framed by the Pintlar, Ruby, and Tobacco Root mountains.

History.... imagine how members of the expedition must have felt when they finally found the Shoshone Indians and changed from boats to horses, giving the expedition new life ... or what it must have been like to find the first gold on Grasshopper Creek in 1862. And, if that's not enough, think of being one of the vigilantes that successfully stopped the plundering gang "The Innocents," headed by Sheriff Henry Plummer. All of these events happened around Dillon, Montana. One can envision the first railroad steam engine roaring into town, frightening horses. Or, how desperate your feelings, if your livelihood came from freighting goods by mule team from Salt Lake City to Butte, and experiencing the "Iron Horse" blasting steam in your face. The history reflects moments in time, one after another.

Small towns along the Missouri River and tributaries have been dressing old western style, offering art galleries, restaurants, and shops for family fun.

The cowtown look adds to the fun of visiting...stop and set a spell!

Downtown Ennis, circa 1997.

ENNIS, MONTANA

Ennis is a superb fishing village built on the Madison River. The strikingly beautiful Madison Mountain Range frames the east side of the valley while to the west, the Gravelly Mountains form the backdrop. Here in cowman's heaven is one of nature's most picturesque valleys, with Ennis as the capital. The town shows off fine restaurants, bookstores, and art galleries, while up and down the blue ribbon trout river, cattle ranches utilize the resources as though the Old West of a hundred years ago were alive and well today.

Small family businesses thrive in the Missouri River Country.

WHERE THE RUBY AND BEAVERHEAD RIVERS MEET

Over the hump where the Beaverhead and Ruby rivers meet lies Twin Bridges, another small town where recreation and cattle spice the cake. Here the Winston Rod Company exemplifies how small occupations can be enlarged to provide jobs for people. The Big Hole River now joins the Beaverhead and the Ruby, forming the Jefferson... to begin a short journey past Whitehall to Three Forks, Montana. The Three Forks Hotel, called Sacajawea, is a monument to the Shoshone woman famous for helping the Lewis and Clark Expedition.

BOZEMAN, MONTANA - 1806

During the return trip from Fort Clatsop, Captain Clark was the first American to gaze into the Gallatin Valley. In the fall of 1807, John Potts and John Colter ventured into the Three Forks of the Missouri River to trap beaver. A small band of Blackfeet warriors jumped the two men. Potts was killed and John Colter was stripped of his clothes. The Indian game of hunting down a man with no weapons or clothes backfired. John Colter, being a hardened outdoorsman from three years on the expedition, managed to outrun the Indians. John killed one Indian brave with his own spear, then ran to the Madison River, hid in a log jam in the water, and finally arrived at Fort Manuel Lisa days later, having walked 250 miles on sore, cactus filled feet.

Downtown Bozeman

JOHN BOZEMAN

For fifty years, the vicious Blackfeet Indians were able to keep all whites out of the Gallatin Valley until gold was discovered in the river drainages nearby. John Marvin Bozeman, born in Georgia in 1837, was one of the early Virginia City miners. John, like many miners, was "a day late and a dollar short" and became discouraged when his gold pan came up empty. But, with the price of flour at $150 per hundred pound sack, he wisely thought farming in the Gallatin Valley might add more gold flakes in his pan than sluicing.

John Bozeman organized a small group of farmers to begin raising wheat, potatoes, cattle, and sheep. John Bozeman, Beall, and Rouse became the first realtors of the area as they laid out a new town with lots for sale in 1864. John envisioned hotels, stores, stage lines, freight depots and a new route into the gold fields from the east. The new town was given the name Bozeman. The Bozeman Trail, also laid out by John Bozeman, followed the Yellowstone River, and trailed around the Bighorn Mountains, through Red Cloud's Sioux country. This route would shorten the trip to Bozeman by several months. "The Bozeman Trail" is thought to have been traversed by 1000 wagons in 1864.

By December, 1864, the town of Bozeman boasted six structures ... one and a half story hotel and others. The hotel quickly became a thriving business, and the 160-acre farms were making more money than most miners. The 1865 crop totaled 20,000 bushels of wheat for local sales.

John Bozeman was a handsome frontier man towering six feet and weighing 200 pounds, attractive to women. Several years later while traveling on a business trip east of Livingston, Montana, John Bozeman was murdered. The blame was placed on five Blackfeet Indians, but the evidence points to some of his business friends. John's indiscretion with wives in Bozeman may have been the cause of his demise.

Montana's premier ski resort, Big Sky, where Chet Huntley, newscaster for NBC, and the Chrysler Corporation began a dream in the 1970's to create a world-class winter sports mecca.

Two political advantages were gained by blaming the Indians ... John was dead and the town asked for and received an 800-man battalion to be stationed for protection. Two forts were set up ... one at Bozeman and Fort Ellis in Livingston 22 miles away. The men were to receive 40 cents a day and rations. The businessmen of Bozeman felt this was a marvelous way to raid the Federal Treasury and prices for everything doubled.

The city of Bozeman sits in the northeastern part of the Gallatin Valley. This beautiful small area is framed by the Bridger Mountains to the northeast, the Gallatin Mountains to the southeast, and the Spanish Peaks to the south and west. The Gallatin alluvial plain has some of the deepest and richest soils found in America and agriculture flourished.

YELLOWSTONE NATIONAL PARK

Fort Ellis was kept intact to protect the settlers and help travelers visit the new Yellowstone National Park which was established in 1872. First, the area was part of the Idaho Territory, but after the Alder Gulch gold discoveries, it became the Montana Territory. Both forks of the Gallatin River flow through Gallatin Valley, then east to help form the headwaters of the Missouri River.

Gradually as politics, counties and statehood were sorted out, the town became a center of Montana economics. The Northern Pacific railroad arrived in the early 1880s, Bozeman and the Gallatin Valley became an attractive area for settlement. In 1880, the population of Bozeman numbered 804 people. Today the number is 38,645, still a small city. Montana State University was established in 1893 as an institution of higher learning, adding to the economy.

Today, Bozeman, complete with medical facilities, a modern airport and first class skiing (Big Sky and Bridger Bowl) is truly a unique place to live. The area is a mecca for all types of outdoor recreation (fly fishing, hunting, snowmobiling, skiing, to name a few).

The old field house, MSU Bozeman, established 1893.

Bozeman Deaconess Medical facilities serve the Gallatin area with up-to-date medical care.

Courtesy of the Grizzly Discovery Center, West Yellowstone

Captain Clark found the "Grizzly Bear" to live up to his Indian reputation "The Terrible" as these bears would stand their ground when approached by these new white men. The first attempt at taking a grizzly to be sent back to Washington was near disaster as the wounded animal sent all scurrying to the river. It took many shots before the grizzly was finally killed.

These small Rocky Mountain valleys offer beauty, quiet living, and diverse outdoor activities.

Agriculture is still the backbone of economics, but small ranch tracts are pushing the old ways aside.

These quiet villages and small towns are ideal for small manufacturing and assembly businesses. And, as more firms discover the advantages of operating here, the character of these valleys will continue to change.

Three cities were wooing the population to become the state capital...Virginia City, Anaconda, and Helena. The swing vote came from the north and east. Helena won, basically, because of its more central location. In 1889, Helena was voted the capital of the new state, Montana.

HELENA, MONTANA

The capital of the fourth largest geographical state of the United States began as gold claims in Last Chance Gulch.

Between the grizzly bears, rattlesnakes, and outlaws, survival of an honest gold miner in 1863 was questionable. Nevertheless, the four Georgians who were headed for the Klondike to seek fortunes decided to take one more chance in Montana.

Reginald Stanley, John Crabb, John Cowan, and D. J. Miller, known as the four Georgians, were headed north to Alaska when they talked

The State Capital of Montana was officially christened November, 1889.

to miners who returned from the Klondike. The story was grim.

The rest is history as they turned back and went prospecting over the hill into the prickly pear country. Last Chance Gulch was properly named as no one would expect the yellow metal to be found there. Here, in a pebbled channel where a small stream happily gurgled down to the valley, the pan came up with enough color to file claims.

The gold was easy but a big old boar grizzly liked to feed on the chokecherries growing along the bottom. The miners needed great care to get along with this old boy. Further down the small stream the water ran into broken rocks where the rattlesnakes were so abundant they seemed everywhere. The lower area was given the auspicious name, rattlesnake. At the place of beginning hung the skin of one of the biggest snakes ever found in Montana. The change into autumn was welcome as the frost caused the denning of the snakes, and the prospectors could pan gold without worry.

Virginia City, the capital of the Montana Territory, was where the big gold strike was found. The extractors took 60 million in gold from the area, and the town of Virginia City felt it should be the capital of the new state of Montana.

Anaconda, Virginia City and Helena were in a struggle to gain enough votes to become the state capital in 1889.

Earlier the vigilantes had cleaned out the outlaws in Virginia City and Helena so either area was considered appealing. Anaconda was the home of the largest copper smelting business in the world. Tycoons, Clark and Daly of the Butte - Anaconda copper district were lobbying hard to have the capital located in their district.

Last Chance Gulch won again as the votes were cast to locate the capital in the more geographical center of the state.

The railroad connected Helena to the rest of the United States and in November 1889, the star was placed where once an old boar grizzly bear called home.

Helena...the struggle of being the early capital was not easy as fires, floods, and corruption plagued the city. The people, now calling Montana home, had come from everywhere. They were tough and resourceful. They fought back to make Last Chance Gulch a place forever theirs.

Today, Last Chance Gulch is a cozy business and shopping district next to the Rocky Mountains and full of memories. The four

Georgians, and Thomas Cruse, Colonel C.A. Broadwater, Samuel Hauser, Cornelius Hedges, and Anton M. Holter were all men able to start with a pick, shovel, and sluice box and had the vision to shape a new country into a better place for others to live.

In the early years, Last Chance Gulch was a rickety old mining town. Now, with major remodeling, the area has shops, office buildings, and is a fun place to visit.

CHARLIE RUSSELL

Hot, sticky middle America was no place for a boy wishing to be a cowboy...

Charlie Russell, born in 1864 in Missouri, seemed destined to be the cowboy and western artist everyone in Montana claimed for a friend. Even as a young boy he dreamed of leaving Missouri to follow his vision of the west...Indians, cows with big horns, horses working cattle, the Grizzly bear, and anything else frontier life could hand out.

His mother and father fought a difficult battle to keep Charlie in school and finally bought him a train ticket to Montana. In 1880, Charlie left Missouri to find work on a sheep

The C.M. Russell Museum in Great Falls, Montana has one of the best collections of his works and on campus is his studio.

beautiful, rugged canyon. Charlie shared Jake's home for several years in a mountain setting most would envy. This country provided Charlie with the inspiration for his early strokes of painting deer, elk, buffalo, and the rocks.

Charlie went home to Missouri but almost as soon as he arrived he was lonesome for the mountains and high valleys which he called home. He took a friend on the train back to Billings, Montana, but the friend became ill and died. Charlie, alone again, started northwest on horseback and chanced upon a big cow outfit needing a horse wrangler. He was hired. For the next eleven years, he lived out his dream as a cowboy, singing to cattle at night, and learning to hold a job in this forlorn country where luck was as tough as you make it.

Charles Marion Russell enjoyed painting and his unique ability to illustrate western life began to pay off. The Utica saloonkeeper commissioned Charlie to do several scenes for him and soon the *Cowboy Artist* became known throughout Montana. He lived the life he painted and he searched for his pictures throughout the frontier. He took time to live with the Indians gathering images he would later paint. He joined pack trips with trappers, hunters, and others venturing into the Rockies. These scenes became the canvas of the west.

Ben Roberts invited Charlie to dinner at his home along with another guest, a young woman named Nancy Cooper. Charlie began having trouble seeing straight and his extra time was spent walking along the Missouri River talking with this Nancy girl. He gave her his horse, Monte, the Paint from the Blackfeet Indian. His friends were shocked

ranch in the new Montana Territory. The last leg of his journey was by stagecoach to Helena, Montana - a wild, wild town filled with mule skinners, cowboys, miners, and other characters which suited Charlie's imagination.

Although he was a gullible kid of sixteen, he had the grit to stick out this country where the workday was daylight to dark and some days even longer, but it took a while for the green to rub off.

Charlie managed to purchase a pinto horse from a Blackfeet Indian and his real western adventure began. Soon he had experiences with attacking Indians as well as the dullness of herding sheep. His adjustment to work carried problems. He was fired as a sheepherder - he was painting while the sheep wandered over the hill.

When things became almost too bleak even for Charlie, an old mountain man, Jake Hoover, took him in. Jake lived in a cabin on the upper Judith River. Spawned from the Little Belt Mountains, the stream meandered northward to the Missouri, the water cut through the limestone uplifts forming a

Courtesy of the Bair Museum, Martinsdale, MT
artist: C.M. Russell

Charlie was everyone's friend..from the bars to aristocrats, and especially the Indians. He felt many injustices were dealt the Native Americans.

knowing the only way he would get his horse back was to marry the girl. They said, "It's settled, Charlie's gone."

Nancy proved to be the turning point in Charlie's life. She became his business manager, organizer, and settled Charlie into a routine, putting the artist's career into high gear. Nancy shifted the price of his pieces from $50 to $300 to $400 and eventually they commanded $10,000!

Charlie was one with Montana and Montana claimed him as its son. Today his paintings, bronzes and old letters are housed in galleries in Helena and Great Falls.

Charlie said, "Ma Nature was my teacher. I'll leave it to you whether she was a good one." Charlie Russell's presence is felt in the names of galleries, bridges, buildings, prints, wildlife refuges, and schools throughout Montana.

THE GREAT FALLS OF THE MISSOURI
The Indians at the winter camp at Fort Mandan knew of the great falls on the Missouri River. When Lewis and Clark arrived in the Fort Benton area on the Missouri, Captain Meriwether Lewis went ahead to scout for the falls. He heard the roar long before finally seeing the first cataract. The Missouri River drops 86 feet forming the first of three falls.

The layers of the Cretaceous period limestone form the bedrock of the middle falls, called Rainbow. The Lewis and Clark portage traveled to the south of these falls.

The underlying geology consists of vast strata of limestone and shales laid down during the Cretaceous Period between 80 and 65 million years ago. Then during the Bull Lake glacial era, the Missouri River was restricted from continuing its northward flow to Hudson Bay, Canada. The river continued erosion of the Rocky Mountains pushing sediments to the plains, but as the glaciers melted, the river again cut down to bedrock. The Missouri River reaching bedrock created three falls ... Black Eagle, Rainbow, and the third, Great Falls. The Missouri River drops more than 400 feet in a distance of ten miles. Spectacular and scenic beyond Captain Lewis's imagination, these falls posed a transportation problem equal to their beauty.

Here in this hot canyon with summer temperatures near 100 degrees, boats and supplies needed to be carried or hoisted up to the canyon rims and around all three falls. This was no small feat with rattlesnakes everywhere and several of the crew members were nearly bitten. The portage, taking nearly two weeks, was estimated to be 18½ miles to White Bear Island, just south of the town now called Great Falls, Montana. Wagon wheels were made from cottonwood rounds. These were pulled across the flats loaded with boats full of supplies. The flats were covered with prickly pear cactus, and was nearly disastrous for the men wearing Indian moccasins. Their feet festered so badly the men could barely walk.

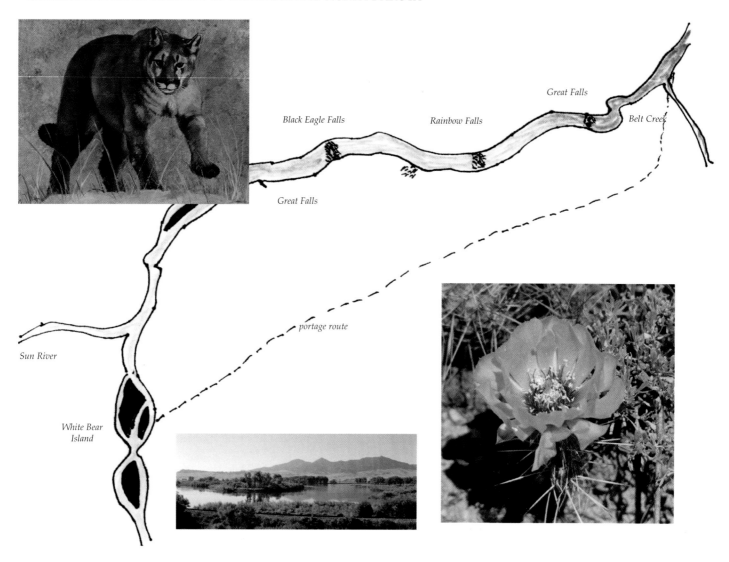

Black Eagle Falls

Rainbow Falls

Great Falls

Belt Creek

Great Falls

portage route

Sun River

White Bear Island

Captain Lewis shot a buffalo when he first arrived at the lower falls, and while deciding how to handle the critter, a large grizzly ambled up to claim the carcass. Lewis, not having his rifle reloaded and in no position to argue, ran for the river. He waded in waist high and turned to face the bear. The grizzly lumbered down to the water's edge, turned, and growled as he departed. Next, Lewis came face to face with a cougar, an unfamiliar animal not seen before. He scared the big cat away with a rifle shot.

At the upper camp, called White Bear Island, a number of unruly grizzlies were troublesome. The grizzly is a territorial animal and resents intrusions, but gradually the bears moved out. Grizzlies, rattlesnakes and the tough portage around the falls nearly ended the expedition at the Great Falls on the Missouri.

GREAT FALLS THE TOWN

The town of Great Falls started as a trade stop between Fort Benton and points south and east. Many European immigrants came by railroad about 1910 and enlarged the trade stop to a bustling city of Montana prominence. A new smelter, part of Anaconda Copper Co., was built and needed laborers. The families immigrated from all parts of Europe.

Homesteaders moved in from 1907 to 1916, and filed on the flats formed by glacial Lake Great Falls. Here a farmer could plant wheat to his heart's content or to the extent of his ability to work hard. They tilled first by horse teams, then tractors, then bigger tractors until time became the only restriction.

Millions of bushels of wheat are harvested each year from the prairies north of Great Falls.

Today, Great Falls is a town blessed by the beauty of the Missouri River, an international airport, major hospital facilities, and a shipping center for grain and cattle. Great Falls is waiting to be discovered again by small manufacturing, offering lifestyles easy and close to nature. Trout fishing is up the canyon on the Missouri; deer and antelope hunting is everywhere out on the prairie flats, and golf is still a bargain. Traveling across town takes only minutes from any point.

Old Fort Benton

Downriver a few miles is old Fort Benton. The railroad bridge reflects the ending of the paddleboats in the 1880's and the beginning of a new transportation era.

113

TOWNS ALONG THE HI-LINE

Choteau, Montana is one of the dinosaur dig sites of the Missouri River area. A unique find of a dinosaur egg nest was discovered not far from here.

Along the hi-line, monster grain elevators were built next to the railroad to store wheat from prairie farms.

The Blackfeet Indian Museum, Browning, Montana.

The old post office and court house, Havre, Montana.

Malta, Montana

Glasgow, Montana

CULBERTSON, MONTANA

Alexander Culbertson, Scotsman, was head bourgeois of Fort Benton, Fort Union, and Fort Sarpy. He was called the King of the High Missouri. His beautiful Indian wife, Natawista, was a Blackfeet Chieftan's daughter. Alex dressed his wife in red velvet, emeralds, rubies, and gold jewelry. Even John James Audubon was so awed by her exceptional beauty that he called her, 'Queen of the High Missouri'.

Toward the end of Alex Culbertson's career, he helped Governor Stevens of the Washington Territory in formulating the major Indian Treaty of 1855, encompassing the Flatheads, Nez Perce, Spokanes, Blackfeet, Cree, Assiniboine, Yankton, and other tribes. This treaty created the landmark clause for Indians giving them dual citizenship. They were citizens of the United States of America and citizens of their sovereign lands. In 1925, Chief Justice Douglas ruled on this clause giving these rights in perpetuity to the Indians.

Alexander Culbertson befriended many world dignitaries who found traveling up the Missouri a special mission. He became close friends with Prince Maxmillian, Carl Bodner, John Audubon, and Father DeSmet.

FAMOUS NAMED TOWNS IN THE MISSOURI RIVER COUNTRY

CUT BANK • PLENTYWOOD • ROUNDUP

Cut Bank named after the creek records some of the coldest temperatures of the United States. Roundup, on the Musselshell, aquired its name in the early years of the longhorn cattle drives.

The town of Plentywood, Montana gained its name sometime in the late 1880's. A small group of cowboys were making camp on the Big Muddy Creek that drains northeastern Montana. The cook was trying unsuccessfully to coax a fire out of some wet buffalo chips. After frustration set in, one of the better known cowpokes, Dutch Henry, in his broken tongue said, "Up creek, two miles is plenty wood." Dutch was given credit for the town's name. In 1905 a post office was awarded to George Bolster's store. This was the official

beginning of the town.

In January 1914, Ford car agent Joe Kavon received fifty two Model T Fords for sale in Plentywood and quickly sold all of them.

Freda Friedrich was born in St. Paul, Minnesota July 31, 1890 as Freda Reedinger. She is now 106 years old and lives in the nursing home. After marrying Edwin Friedrich, Freda and Edwin traveled by Great Northern Railroad to the Plentywood country in December 1917. They settled on a farm in Antelope, Montana, a few miles south of Plentywood. The family had filed on several homestead claims totaling 800 acres to raise wheat and some cattle.

Edwin died 16 years later and Freda raised their five children, four boys and a daughter, alone. Freda talked of cold winters out on the farm and about her oldest son being killed in a hunting accident. She said they were the kind to "stick it out" regardless of prices, crop failures, or bad weather. Freda says "I've lost count of the number of grandchildren and great-grandchildren, but I know I have three great great great grandchildren." Some of her grandsons are still on the farm raising wheat, barley, and cattle.

JORDAN, MONTANA 1899

The "Big Dry" is situated on alkali flats, grassy knolls and a stretch of miles in the middle of the Montana Territory. During the early snow melt or a rainy season, the Big Dry Creek would carry water to the Missouri River. In 1899, a U.S. Post Office was awarded to the town, consisting of only a home... trading post one hundred miles north of Miles City.

The town was named for Arthur Jordan. He traveled from England and visited the "Big Dry" country on a hunting trip several years before. He stated that one day he would come back and settle there. When he returned, he built a home in the flood plain of Big Dry Creek. Not knowing the weather of this area, the building would later have to be moved. The home was located halfway between Miles City and the Missouri Breaks. Miles City had been a riverboat dock, but became a civilized cowtown with a railroad depot. Goods unloaded at the railroad docks would be freighted by 12-horse teams into the back country. Arthur Jordan's home, a hundred miles to the north, became a way station store, and started one of the meanest small towns in the west. Cowboys would stop for a meal, gloves, whiskey and ammunition ... mostly for whiskey. After dinner, they would throw the tin plates into the air and challenge each other to shoot holes in them. In the "Big Dry's" early years, before the existence of Jordan, the country was cattle and sheep range. Migratory herds of livestock would be grazed

by Hall Diteman

Freighting goods from Miles City to Jordan because of the remote area, lasted well into the 1900's. The 12-horse teams struggled in bad weather to supply the trading post called Jordan.

through, harvesting the grass. After Jordan set up his temporary store, cowboys such as Long-Haired Charlie, Ed Curl, and Billy Sanders would come looking for a good time. Following a poker game, the fun would often turn raw, and the first fourteen grave markers read "Died a tragic death."

So, from the first post office in 1899 to 1910, Jordan, Montana had the reputation "come and we'll bury you". This fate might not be as bad as staying in the hotel where bed bugs would take a big share of blood each night.

It took some time for Jordan to heal from the early gunshot wounds, to having a fine dinosaur museum showing the Tyranosaurus Rex bones dug north of town. Today, Jordan is a quiet town, a wide spot on Highway 200 where one can travel to Circle, Miles City, or Winnett, Montana. The town's history is dubious and in the early years, if you did not die young from gunshot, you would probably go lonesome crazy before you could get out of there. The surrounding country looks much the same as it did 150 years ago. Distance is the horizon of a hundred miles or so. In between, you might spot several antelope or a cow tuckin' away high protein grass for fall fat. Here is nowhere, and everywhere, so bring your lunch.

The Little Missouri and North Dakota

The headwaters of the Little Missouri begin west of Devil's Tower, the first national monument set aside for visitors during President Theodore Roosevelt's administration.

CHAPTER 10
The Little Missouri and North Dakota

The Missouri River is called the "Big Muddy." Rightfully the Little Missouri should be the "Little Muddy." Continued erosion from the desert regions of Wyoming and Montana keeps the river bottom constantly moving. The Little Missouri forms the boundary between the Badlands and the continental prairies and farmlands of the Midwest. Theodore Roosevelt spent a share of his life being an outdoorsman, cowpoke, and ranch owner, his fondness for the area encouraged preservation. Part of Roosevelt's conservation legacy was to restore the wildlife to the area.

Prairie Dog barking

Cottontail

When the Wisconsin Glacier moved down from Canada, it profoundly affected the Little Missouri River system, causing the river to divert from the Hudson Bay joining the Missouri River to flow eastward to the Mississippi. Also, during the Bull Lake Ice Age, the glacial flows and movement of sediments caused pileups of materials which later eroded into the fascinating hills and ravines in the Little Missouri River badlands.

LITTLE MISSOURI RIVER

This area has undergone many transformations since the mountain building sixty-five million years ago. The geologic formation of Fort Union group spread out over this area from the water flows off the Rocky Mountains. The Little Missouri continued to cut through the geologic deposits, carving out its canyon. Erosion continues to create an everchanging look year after year.

During the Lewis and Clark Expedition up the Missouri River, one of the first tributaries was this river, flowing in from the south. The Little Missouri is still in transition, moving mud and silt downstream. This action continues from the prehistoric origins when the land rose above the ocean floor and square miles were covered with cinder and ash from volcanoes. During these early geologic times, the Little Missouri country would flood, allowing sediments to spread, forming eastern Montana, northeastern Wyoming, parts of South Dakota, and western North Dakota. Particles held in suspension floated down river to the Gulf of Mexico, but those deposited formed alluvial flats wherever the terrain would allow. These floods and the constant erosion from the mountains also created swamps and lakes. Channels of running river waters gradually exposed layer after layer of sediments, coal seams, and rock crystallization. The make up of the Little Missouri Canyon shows from beginning to end how volatile young rivers are.

Erosion of Little Missouri sediments has created many, many oddities throughout Theodore Roosevelt National Park.

The pile up of sedimentary materials and the constant re-erosion has created one of the most spectacular natural settings in the continental United States... The Badlands. Thousands of years of swamps producing coal beds and oil deposits are illustrated in the layers of materials exposed in the Badlands.

The river begins in the northeast corner of Wyoming between Devil's Tower and the Powder River. This is an area almost forgotten and nondescript in character until the eroded canyon begins to take shape.

Theodore Roosevelt discovered the badlands while on a hunting trip around the turn of the century. He became so enamored with its unique beauty and the river's carvings, he decided to purchase a ranch near Medora, North Dakota. Theodore Roosevelt National Park had its beginning in 1947 and is comprised of two units, North and South. Other set aside lands under government supervision are the National Grasslands along the Little Missouri River.

During the time when President Roosevelt was concerned with the river area, overgrazing and the killing of wild game was unchecked. He wanted this beautiful and unique area to return to a pristine state. Visitors touring the park today can see animals and plants in their natural setting. Buffalo, mule deer, wild mustangs, bighorn sheep and countless small creatures live in balance with nature and have overcome some of their fear of man.

The real beauty of this natural formation demonstrates how a small river system can transform a landscape into a setting where with every hour of passing daylight, the scene changes. The park and national grasslands flow together, illustrating how various aspects of agriculture, tourism, and extractive resource industries can harmoniously work together.

Theodore Roosevelt stated, "I may never have been president without my experiences in North Dakota." In these western badlands, he was a cowboy, hunter, and cattle baron. Here he lived up to his image of the rough, tough man who lived close to nature. His North Dakota experiences forged his conservation views which led to the formation of the U. S. Forest Service called The Antiquities Act of 1906. Under this act, fifty one wildlife refuges, eighteen national monuments, and five more national parks were created. Montana's Charles M. Russell Wildlife Refuge is one of the units occupying portions of the Missouri Breaks with the Fort Peck Reservoir.

Water, the master artist, creates faces of Earth's history shown throughout the Little Missouri River drainage.

WILLISTON BASIN

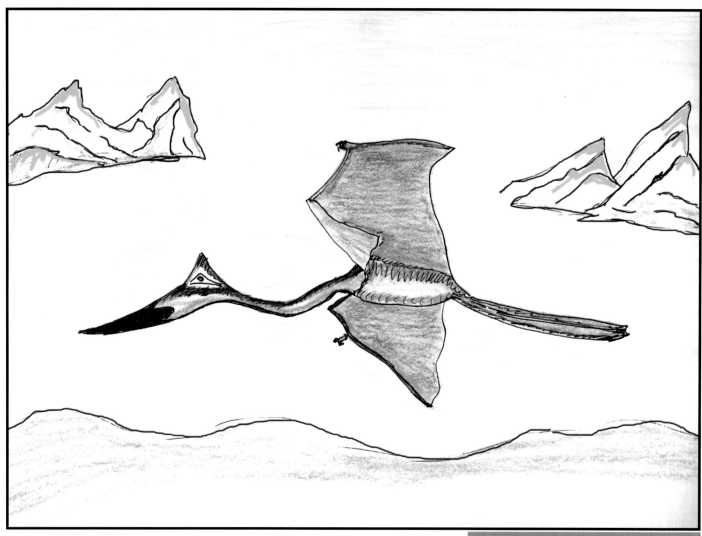

During the time of "flying lizards," Pteranodons, shallow seas and swamps were allowing tiny crustacea, algae, and diatoms to create the oil fields of the Williston Basin. This oil field is the most productive of Montana and North Dakota.

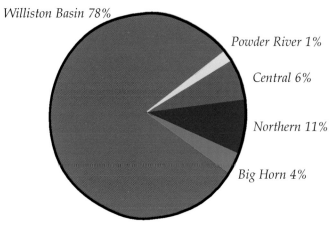

Williston Basin 78%

Powder River 1%

Central 6%

Northern 11%

Big Horn 4%

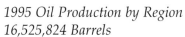

1995 Oil Production by Region
16,525,824 Barrels

Garrison Dam forms Lake Sacagewa in North Dakota, and along with the Canyon Ferry and Fort Peck Reservoirs help regulate the water flow of the Missouri River. This stream flow regulation has changed the ecosystems of the river drainage and Bismarck has no massive floods today.

BISMARCK, NORTH DAKOTA

The capital city has evolved through several metamorphoses since its beginning. LeSieur De La Verendrye visited the Mandan Indian village across the river in 1738, and from that time on trading became part of life along the Missouri River.

The next major event was the Lewis and Clark Expedition spending the winter with the Mandan, Arikara, and Gros Ventre tribes in 1804-1805.

Shortly after the return of Lewis and Clark, the American Fur Company established Fort Mitchell near the present location of Bismarck.

First, the steamboats came only to this fort. Then, in 1832 Fort Union at the mouth of the Yellowstone was available to receive riverboat traffic. Later, in 1859, the boat traffic ventured to Fort Benton and Miles City.

The Dakota Territory was established in 1861, but prior to this, Bismarck was a trading port, fuel stop for riverboats, and travel into the Montana Territory. Bismarck was second only to Dodge City, Kansas as a place where your coffin might come soon. The composition of people... riverboat traffic, fur traders, hunters, and cowmen created a tough western town.

The railroad came in 1874 and the first bridge across the Missouri River was set on frozen ice. Following the railroad came the homesteaders peaking in 1884 with 11 million acres issued to settlers. Then came statehood in 1889.

The first capitol burned in 1932 and soon the present building was constructed.

A reflection of the Missouri River, at the river park in Bismarck, North Dakota.

The town began in 1865 with several buildings and the First Presbyterian Church was built in 1873. The First National Bank opened in 1872 giving Bismarck its official beginning. Incorporation of the city was January 14, 1875 with the Edmund Hackett as Mayor-Elect.

The Missouri Drainage is an area of several hundred thousand square miles. When weather conditions were right, the floods would visit Bismarck wreaking havoc. Today the flood control dams of Canyon Ferry, Fort Peck, and Garrison keep excessive waters stored for later release.

Today Bismarck, North Dakota is a beautiful city on the banks of the Missouri. Several airlines serve the city with modern transportation in keeping with its early image.

The capitol of North Dakota.

In the Missouri River Country the unusual is usual...look for rare finds of nature, hidden in the wide outdoors and in the little shops along the way.

courtesy of Harmon Rock Shop, Savage, MT

Yellowstone River agates show dendrites of brownish mineral deposits. Chalcedony and agate form in cavities by precipitation from solutions.

Missouri River sapphires are formed in diatremes of molten rock slowly cooling and forming crystals. Areas where these crystals are found are Sri Lanka, Cashmir, Afghanistan, Queensland, New South Wales, and Montana.

CONCLUSION
A Look Forward at the Missouri River Country

Small animals...rabbits, squirrels, need habitats where they can have a home. When the countryside is clean of rubble and tall grasses, these creatures have no place to go.

CONCLUSION

Rural America is in transition and as this face changes, the surrounding environment will need a different artist. America is a country of private property rights, families owning their homes, farms, or ranches. Businesses can be either family or individually owned. Many other ownerships are also part of the American enterprise system.

The government, by the Constitution, is a servant of the people. As rural America changes, this concept will be stretched. During the 50's, 60's, and 70's, small family farms grew larger as machinery allowed owners to accomplish more work with fewer people. The wide open spaces and beauty of the West has attracted people from all areas of the United States and Europe. However, in current times,

as ownership of these big ranches change from generation to generation, these visitors have the opportunity to purchase the land. They come to establish deluxe family units and these new estates are not intended to provide the family with an income. This proliferation of country villas built with outside money significantly alters land values. Soon, working farms and ranches, dependent on cattle or wheat sales, cannot support either the new elevated tax base nor produce the income needed to pay for the rearranged economics.

In the Missouri River Country, many areas remain desolate, foreboding, and far from cities. These lands have not, as yet, been attractive real estate for this clientele. But, as one travels closer to the beauty of the mountains with clear spring-fed streams, small country ranches come into view. This new concept of living, where money comes from other than natural resources or growing crops, is changing the established ways of life.

Today, these new land uses are pressure cooking the family farm or ranch, and the very fiber of living in rural America. The land transfer cost of estate taxes and higher values per acre are helping shut the door on the custom of proudly owning a spread in the Rocky Mountain country.

When the century ends it will be nearly 200 years from Lewis and Clark's first look at the Missouri River Country. Untouched for billions of years, the Missouri River Country was transformed almost overnight by gold, copper, wheat, and cattle to boost a young country into world-wide dominance. It is now time to assess growth, quality of life, and how to sustain an economy where families can share the American way.

The environment of the Rocky Mountains, Missouri back country and the badlands of the Little Missouri is extremely fragile. People from every corner of America and the world come to spend a few moments trout fishing, looking at buffalo, elk, bighorn sheep, or watch a geyser spouting into the sky. The challenge will be to protect and maintain the pristine atmosphere, yet carefully allow visitors from every walk of life to have the opportunity to dream he is "Mountain Man" Jim Bridger seeing the majestic splendor of the Missouri River Country for the very first time.

The technology changes from Lewis and Clark pulling their boats up the Missouri in 1805...to
  • wood-fired steamboats in 1832
  • coal-fired railroad engines in 1890
  • gasoline-fired Model T Fords 1920
  • jet-fired airplanes in 1950
  • rocket-fired spaceships in 1960
  • hydrogen-fired spaceships after 2000

All challenge the ability to understand how this could happen in just 200 short years, and what is yet to follow. But while we can advance in the field of computers, rockets and communications, the world of human relations lags behind. The next one hundred years will be truly exciting. The dovetailing of our many factions with a country in transition will take everyone's concentration to build solid growth and homes for our children.

Europe has solved some of these problems by creating central villages with farm owners traveling out to work the land. Here in America we have allowed helter-skelter visiting rights to public lands. The national parks and forest service are considering fee visitation, charging so many dollars for each time one visits the mountains. Some feel this is discriminatory to lower-income people, and possibly a quota system would be more equitable for controlling the number of footsteps into these fragile areas. This would also allow spreading the visitors more equally across these western lands.

These decisions need to be based on the premise that private property rights, constitutional values, and the individual still reign supreme in America. How public and private lands fit into living in the United States and still preserving small plants and animals will be the indicator of how well we are accomplishing these goals.

Glossary

Agate-Chalcedony: A hard rock composed of silicate and other minerals formed into very tight small crystals. Sometimes forming beautiful expressions.

Altyn Limestone Formation: An exposure of rock found in Glacier National Park, often called dolomite.

Appaloosa: The horse developed by the Nez Perce Indians from an early European breed. Very intelligent, obedient, and fast.

Appekunny Formation: An exposure of rock found in Glacier National Park.

Archean: oldest rock; formed before most life on earth.

Badlands: Broken rough lands formed by washed sediments easily eroded.

Batholith: Large mass of granite covering an area larger than 40 square miles.

Basalt: Dark stone from a volcanic flow; often hardened into columns.

Bentonite: Clay formed from collected volcanic ash and usually sodium from a shallow sea.

Bering Straits: Tip of Alaska reaching toward Asia where during the Ice Age, migration of humans into North America may have occurred.

Bull Lake Ice Age: Time when glacier moved southward from Alaska and Canada, 70,000 to 130,000 years ago.

Caldera: The area or depression inside an inactive volcano.

Cambrian Era: Time of earth's beginning when possibly first life appeared.

Cambrian, Ordovician, Silurian, Devonian, Mississippian, Pennsylvanian and Permian periods: See Earth Age Chart.

Chinook: Indian name for the warm, winter wind descending from the mountains.

Chugwater: soft, red rock formation of the Triassic time.

Climate Zones: Temperature and rainfall variations.

Compression: The outer plates of the earth's crust moving into each other causing mountain building.

Continental Plate: Large blocks of rock and land areas, part of the earth's crust.

Core: Part of the interior of the earth called the center - very heavy and dense.

Cretaceous: see Earth Age Chart.

Crust: The earth's outer layer - lithosphere.

Crustaceans: Small sea creatures, oyster, Brachiopods, etc.

Cyclonic: Movement of air masses in a circular pattern.

Desert: Area of scant vegetation and rainfall.

Diatremes: Igneous intrusions cooled underground, composed of peridotite and other crystals.

Dike: Separation in the earth's surface where magma flows to the surface filling cracks. Often called igneous intrusions.

Dredge: A large machine turning stream bed rock to find gold.

Eocene Epoch: See Earth Age Chart.

Faults: Separation of areas of the earth's crust moving up or down.

Fossil: remains of a prehistoric creature.

Geyser: Super heated water exploded out of a deep crevasse (both steam and water).

Glacial Lake: Lake created by both glacial melt and stream flow.

Glacier: Large ice field.

Gneiss: Metamorphic rock with coarse grains, sometimes banded; can expose minerals of quartz and feldspar.

Granite Batholiths: Upthrust of molten rock hardening into granite.

Granite: Intrusive igneous rock often pink in color.

Grinnell Formation: A red colored rock formation found in Glacier National Park.

Igneous: Rock formed deep in the earth, called fire rock or molten in formation and crystalized as it cools.

Glossary

Indian Mythology: Beliefs of a spiritual nature in Indian society.

Jurassic: See Earth Age Chart.

Limestone: Rock formed from sediment having an abundance of skeletons of sea creatures.

Lithosphere: Earth's crust 4 miles to 40 miles thick.

Louisiana Purchase: Area of land purchased from France in 1803, approximately 800,000 acres.

Magma: Melted rock found in mantle becomes lava at the earth surface.

Mantle: Inner part of earth where molten magma slowly circulates.

Mesozoic: see Earth Age Chart.

Metamorphic: Rock created from heat and pressure deep within the earth.

Miocene: see Earth Age Chart.

Mountain Laramide Orogeny: Time of mountains rising 100 million to 65 millions years in the past.

Ordovician: See Earth Age Chart.

Ore: Any rock profitable to mine for a sellable material.

Pacific plate: Part of lithosphere formed when the Pacific floor began separating.

Paleo: Time of early prehistoric Indian life of North America.

Plate: A segment of the lithosphere.

Paleocene: see Earth Age Chart.

Paleozoic-Mesozoic eras: See Earth Age Chart.

Palladium: Metal used in industry, especially for catalytic convertors for automobiles.

Plate stacking: Compression pushing sedimentary strata positions from horizontal to vertical.

Platinum: Precious metal used in industry, especially computer conductors.

Portage: A transfer of goods around a difficult area of a river.

Pre-Cambrian Era: Time of earth's very beginning - possibly no life.

Pteranodons: A flying dinosaur of the prehistoric time before the Rocky Mountain formation.

Quartz Rock: White crystal rock often having gold depositories.

Rhyolite: Reddish stone from a volcanic flow.

Sandstone: Soft rock of pressed sand.

Sapphires: Hard crystals found only in a few places in the world. Sapphires and rubies are very similar. Missouri River sapphires come in many colors and are formed in diatremes.

Sedimentary strata: layer of rock formed from sediment, then called sandstone.

Sediments: Materials washed by water and settled mud, sand, etc.

Shonkinite: A type of dark lava prevalent in the Belt and Highwood Mountains of Montana.

Smelter: A factory where metals are separated into pure forms.

Subterranean: Name given to areas deep in earth.

Travertine: Limestone rock from minerals of a hot spring.

Triassic, Jurassic, and Cretaceous: See Earth Age Chart.

Tyranosaurus Rex: Large meat eating dinosaur.

Uplift: The movement of a continental plate during compression.

Vein: A collection of distinctive rock collected along a fracture - often valuable to mine.

Vigilantes: Organized group of men to bring justice to the frontier.

Volcanoes: The crust fractures allowing magma to flow to the surface forming a mountain with an eruptive center.

Yucca: A cactus plant growing on rocky slopes of the prairie.

Bibliography

Abarr, Don. 1989. Hoofbeats on the Wind. Columbus, MT: The Stillwater Sun.

Alstad, Ken. 1994. Savvy Sayin's. Tucson, AZ: Ken Alstad Company.

Alt, David D. and Donald W. Hyndman. 1972. Roadside Geology of the Northern Rockies. Missoula, MT: Mountain Press Publishing.

Anderson, Bob. 1994. Beartooth Country, Montana's Absaroka and Beartooth Mountains. Helena, MT: Montana Magazine.

Anneke, Jan Boden. 1984. Montana, A Pictorial History. The Donning Company Publishers, 5659 Virginia Beach Boulevard, Norfolk, VA 23502.

Ballantine and Ballantine, Editors. 1993. The Native Americans, an Illustrated History. Turner Publishing, Inc., 1050 Techwood Drive NW, Atlanta, GA 30318.

Bowers, Alfred W. 1991. Mandan Social and Ceremonial Organization. University of Idaho Press.

British Museum. 1985. Dinosaurs and Their Living Relatives. London and Cambridge, Great Britain: British Museum and Press Syndics of Cambridge University.

Brown, Bruce and Lane Morgan. 1990. The Miracle Planet. New York: Gallery Books.

Capps and Editors of Time Life Books. 1973. The Indians. Time-Life Books, New York.

Catlin, George. North American Indians, Manner and Customs. David Bogue, 86 Fleet Street , Lake Tilt and Bogue, 1844.

Clawson, Roger. 1996. Montana, a State to Treasure. The Prose Works.

Clokey, Richard M. 1980. William H. Ashley. University of Oklahoma Press, Norman and London.

Dannen, Kent and Donna Dannen. 1981. Rocky Mountain Wildflowers. Estes Park, CO: Tundra Publications.

Dempsey, Hugh A. Crowfoot, Chief of the Blackfeet. Norman, Oklahoma: University of Oklahoma Press, 1972.

Department of Natural Resources and Conservation for the State of Montana. August 1995. Montana Oil and Gas Annual Review. Vol. 38.

Dippie, Brian W. 1982. Remington & Russell. Austin, TX: University of Texas Press.

Dippie, Brian W. "Government Patronage: Catlin, Stanley, and Eastman." Montana, Vol. 44, No. 4 (Autumn 1994): 40-53.

Ewers, John C. 1958. The Blackfeet Raiders on the Northwestern Plains. University of Oklahoma Press, Norman and London.

Ewing, Sherm. 1995. The Ranch. A Modern History of the North American Cattle Industry. Missoula, MT: Mountain Press Publishing.

Feldman, Robert. 1985. The Rockhound's Guide to Montana. Helena, MT: Falcon Press.

Fritz, William J. 1985. Roadside Geology of the Yellowstone Country. Missoula, MT: Mountain Press Publishing.

Gordon, Albie, Margaret Lehfeldt, and Mary Morsanny. 1971. Down in Golden Valley. Visalia, CA: American Yearbook Company.

Graves, F. Lee. 1994. Montana's Fur Trade Era. Helena, MT: American and World Geographic Publishing.

Hager, Mark. 1970. Fossils of Wyoming. Laramie, WY: University of Wyoming.

Harris, Burton. 1993. John Colter. Lincoln, NE: University of Nebraska Press.

Hasrick, Royal B. 1976. Cowboys and Indians. Octopus Books Limited, 59 Grosvenor Street, London, WI.

Highland, Geneva. 1960. Big Dry Country.

Holterman, Jack. 1987. King of the High Missouri. The Saga of the Culbertsons. Falcon Press Publishing Co., Inc.

Jassem, Kate. Sacajawea, Wilderness Guide. Troll Associates.

Lacey, Theresa Jensen. 1995. The Blackfeet Indians of North America. Chelsea House Publishers.

Lagerson, David R. and Darwin R. Spearing. 1988. Roadside Geology of Wyoming. Missoula, MT: Mountain Press Publishing.

Lambert, Diagram Group. 1988. Geology, the Field Guide to Facts on File, Inc., an Infobase Holding Company.

Lanford, Nathaniel P. 1996. Vigilante Days and Ways. American and World Geographic Publishing, Helena, Montana.

Larpenteur, Charles. 1989. Forty years a Fur Trader on the Upper Missouri. 1833-1872. Paul L. Hedren, Editor. University of Nebraska Press, Lincoln and London.

Lessem, Don and Glut, Donald I. 1993. The Dinosaur Society. Random House, Inc., New York.

McDowell, Bart. "CM Russell Cowboy Artist". National Geographic, Vol. 169, No. 1 (January 1986): 46-50.

McRae, W. C. and Judy Jewell. 1994. Montana Handbook. Chico, CA: Moon Publications.

Meloy, Mark. 1986. The Mountain Ranges of Eastern Montana, Islands on the Prairie. Helena, MT: Montana Magazine.

O'Brien, Mary Barmeyer. 1995. Bright Star in the Big Sky. Helena, MT: Falcon Press.

O'Hara, Pat. 1991. Wilderness Scenario, Peaceful Images of the Wild. American and World Geographic Publishing, P. O. Box 5630, Helena, Montana 59604.

Paladin and Baucus. 1983-1996. Helena. An Illustrated History. Montana Historical Society Press, Helena, Montana.

Pellant, Chris, Phillips, Roger. (1990). Rocks, Minerals and Fossils of the World. Little, Brown and Company. Boston, Toronto, London.

Popovich, John A. 1986. The Voice of the Curlew. J. K. Ralston's Story of His Life. The J. K. Ralston Studio, Inc.

Rattenbury, Richard C. 1993. Packing Iron: Gunleather of the West. Millwood, NY: Zon International Publishing Company.

Raup, Earhart, Whipple and Carrara. 1983. Geology - Along Going-to-the-Sun Road, Glacier National Park, Montana. U. S. Geological Survey - National Park Service, Glacier Natural History Association.

Readers Digest. 1978. America's Fascinating Indian Heritage - The First Americans - Their Customers, Art, History, and How They Lived. The Readers Digest Association.

Reese, Rick. 1991. Greater Yellowstone the National Park and Adjacent Wildlands. Helena, MT: Montana Magazine.

Rhodes, Frank H. T., Herbert S. Zim, and Paul R. Shaffer. 1962. Fossils. New York: Golden Press.

Rostud, Lee. 1992. Fourteen Cents and Seven Green Apples. Life of Charles Bair.

Roundup, Montana, Museum Historical Research Committee, comp. 1974. Roundup on the Musselshell. Roundup, MT: The Roundup Record-Tribune.

Russell, Osborne. Aubrey L. Haimes and Norma Tirrell, eds. 1955. Rocks, Minerals, and Fishes of the World. Lincoln, NE: University of Nebraska Press.

Sandoz, Mari. 1978. The Battle of the Little Bighorn. University of Nebraska Press, Lincoln and London.

Scriver, Bob. 1992. The Blackfeet Artist of the Northern Plains. Published by The Lowell Press, Inc., Kansas City.

Stegner, Wallace. 1954. Beyond the Hundredth Meridian. New York: Penguin Books.

Taylor & Taylor, Sturtevant, William. 1991. The Native Americans - The Indigenous People of North America. Smithmark Publishers, 16 East 32nd Street, New York, NY 10019.

Thomas, Phillip Drennon. "Slice of Heart: Holiday Greetings from Charles M. Russell." Southwest Art, Vol. 24, No. 7 (December 1994): 46-50.

Thomas, David Hurst, Jay Miller, Richard White, Peter Nabokov, and Philip J. Deloria. 1993. The Native Americans: An Illustrated History. Atlanta, GA: Turner Publishing, Inc.

Thompson, Ida. 1982. National Audubon Society Field Guide to North American Fossils. New York: Alfred A. Knopf.

Time-Life Books, Editors. 1993. The Wild West. Warner Books, A Time Warner Company, 1271 Avenue of the Americas, New York, NY 10020.

Tirrell, Norma. 1995. Montana. Oakland, CA: Compass American Guides.

Van West, Carroll. 1986. A Traveler's Companion to Montana History. Helena, MT: Montana Historical Society Press.

Vestal, Stanley. 1946. Jim Bridger, Mountain Man. Lincoln, NE: University of Nebraska Press.

White, Richard S. and Robert E. Short, eds. 1988. Achieving Efficient Use of Rangeland Resources: Papers Presented at the Fort Keogh Research Symposium. Bozeman, MT: Montana State University Agricultural Experiment Station.

Wilkinson, Todd. 1991 Greater Yellowstone National Forests. Helena, MT: Falcon Press.

Index

Index

Introduction of the Author - Synopsis

THE ROCKY MOUNTAIN SERIES

Published by

"MONTANA SPEAKS"

This series is a photo-journal with written expression both as captions and text, illustrating the northern Rocky Mountains 1) history, 2) geology, 3) geography, and 4) current affairs

Book One-The Yellowstone River Country of Montana and Wyoming is now published.

Book Two-The Missouri River Country of Montana and North Dakota is the second book in the Rocky Mountain series.

Book Three will be the Columbia River Country of Montana and Idaho.

Book Four will be the Snake River Country of Wyoming, Idaho, and eastern Oregon.

These books illustrate how geology is the foundation of geography and how geography dictates history. These sciences, in tandem, create the activities people engage in while living in an area.

Book Two, the Missouri River Country of Montana and North Dakota, visits the Indians, history, and the influence of the Lewis and Clark Expedition of 1804-1806. History and activities are followed through to the source of the Missouri River. Men, towns, railroad, and homesteaders are visited throughout the 200 year history period.

Enjoy the rendition of Thomas Jefferson, Captain Lewis, Captain Clark, Henry Plummer, Chief Joseph and other characters forming the history of the Missouri River Country.

ABOUT THE AUTHOR

Tom Thayer lived in Oregon from 1941 until 1981 when he moved to Billings to continue in the business of insurance and agricultural financial planning.

During life in Oregon, Tom attended Western Oregon College of Education and completed his master's degree from the University of Oregon in 1954.

After coaching and teaching in the Oregon school systems for thirteen years, his amateur photography hobby became his occupation. Tom worked with CBS News for the next 14 years. During this time, Tom's work took him to cover the Alaskan earthquake, Vietnam, Kruschev's Canadian trip, and many political stories with Rockefeller, Robert Kennedy, Nixon, McGovern, and others. During this time his scope was broadened with travel and discussion with commentators like Charles Kuralt, Bill Kurtis, Dan Rather, Bill Plante, Ike Pappas, and others.

Now retirement has rolled around and it's time to expand his creative ideas. The Rocky Mountain books are photo-journals covering the topics of early Indians, fur traders, and trappers, settlements and is interspersed with the geology and geography. The geology covers the formation of the Rocky Mountains and how this happening created the present climate. The geology also is responsible for the natural resources of timber, metals, oil, and recreation.

From the standpoint of reading and viewing materials of this area there seems to be an unquenchable demand. The feeling is most books deal with a single topic showing more of the beauty and not how we live with the mountains, rivers, and countryside, the theme of which may easily be "We live with the environment."

The books look at the mountain areas of the Northern Rockies, including Glacier National Park and the Yellowstone National Park. The books are illustrated with volcanic drawings and photographs and the text explains how this affected the surrounding geography.

The Missouri River Country is a broad area of the north central United States, and its history and contribution is a rich inheritance. This book should be a delight and an enticement to come visit, learning is fun as you explore the rich visualization of beautiful America.